The Book of Signs

For Kim

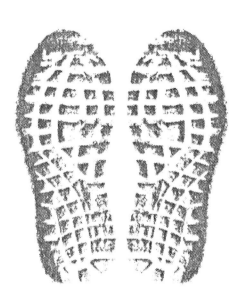

The Book of Signs

A Crowdsourced Field Guide

For

Followers of Jesus

By

Thomas E. Ingram

linen

© 2014

linenpublishing.com

The Book of Signs: A Crowdsourced Field Guide for Followers of Jesus

ISBN 978-0-9908486-2-2

Version 1.0

Published by Linen Publishing

www.linenpublishing.com

Table of Contents

Dedication

Anyone who knows Leonard Sweet, has heard him speak, or read any his books will have little difficulty believing that bouncing around in Len's head are enough ideas to fill several lifetimes. The genesis of this book was one of those ideas.

I had known of Len Sweet's work for several years before I met him at a conference author's book table. Book signing tables can be lonely places for authors and so Len had time to engage in a little conversation. Our discussion was centered on what you might imagine, but I left the table knowing that Len Sweet and I met for a reason that day; we became friends.

This friendship resulted in my enrolling in the Doctor of Ministry in Semiotics and Future Studies program at George Fox Evangelical Seminary of which Len Sweet was (and is) the lead mentor. During my time there, I was honored to serve as his teaching assistant.

At the first gathering of our cohort, Len asked a question: "How would you all like to help me write a book?" Here was the idea. The book would somehow be a collaboration in which whoever wanted to participate would share in the task of generating a list of the top 100 words that make us Christian…and that was that.

As Len's teaching assistant, I felt a certain responsibility to figure out how to make this happen. Crowdsourcing seemed a perfect solution. I contacted a company called Ideascale[1] that created and maintained a platform on which individuals or organizations could set up their own crowdsourcing sites. They

_____

[1] www.ideascale.com

graciously allowed us an educational license for our project and we were ready to begin.[2]

After the crowdsourcing research was complete, I compiled the information and forwarded it to Len who promptly said, "What you have given me is research that should become the topic of your dissertation"…and so it was. He also suggested that after graduation, the two of us work together to complete the book based on this research.

As time went by, the book went through several variations on its path to publication. But, ultimately Len came to the conclusion he was not going to be able to commit the time to this book it needed and offered it up to me to complete and make my own.

While I am grateful and honored to place The Book of Signs before you, this book will never be completely my own. Len birthed the original vision. Len provided the social media clout to announce and engage people to participate. And, Len's confidence in me inspired me to complete this work.

And so, with great humility and pride, I dedicate The Book of Signs to my friend (and someday co-author) Leonard Sweet.

---

[2] You will find more information on crowdsourcing and how the project came together in the Prologue.

Prologue

Crowdsourcing – An Introduction

What if there was an approach to problem solving that, when used properly, tended to generate higher quantities of more robust potential solutions? If there were, wouldn't we expect to see the public and private sectors doing their best to leverage the benefits of this methodology to their respective advantages? Well, there is such a strategy and this is exactly what we are seeing as businesses, both large and small, attempt to utilize a problem solving strategy academics are calling distributed co-creation,[3] more commonly known as crowdsourcing.

In the simplest of definitions, crowdsourcing is a process in which a crowd (a group of self-selected[4] individuals) works together to find a solution to a problem. While a variety of factors contribute to effective crowdsourcing, one of the primary contributors to its ability to uncover innovative solutions seems to be attributable to the advantages associated with diversity in these problem-solving groups. Diversity in this scenario refers to individuals with diverse backgrounds, diverse understandings, and diverse approaches to problem solving. The toolbox is a good metaphor to help us better understand how this works.

Each of us likely has a toolbox of some sort at home. The tools in this toolbox enable us to take on certain projects; to solve certain problems. A

---

[3] Scott E. Page, *The Difference: How the Power of Diversity Creates Better Groups, Firms, Schools, and Societies (New Edition)* (Princeton: Princeton University Press, 2008).

[4] Karim R. Lakhani and Jill A. Panetta, "The Principles of Distributed Innovation," *Innovations: Technology, Governance, Globalization* 2, no. 3 (2007): 105.

hammer enables something different than a screwdriver. A socket set makes possible tasks in which the hammer or screwdriver would be less than useful. And, if one needed to create a precisely sized hole in a piece of wood, having no drill in the toolbox would prove quite detrimental.

This metaphor is applicable to the matter at hand in that each of us possesses a cognitive toolbox containing a variety of problem solving tools.[5] Some cognitive toolboxes hold years of experience in a particular area. Others might be stocked with knowledge in a seemingly unrelated discipline. While a different group of us might have tools that cause us to lean more heavily toward technological solutions, just to name a few.

Over time, we tend to become proficient with our particular tool set (or approach) which predisposes us to view problem solving primarily through the lens of these tools. It is easy for us to assume our particular tool set or approach is applicable to every situation because these tools are what we know and what we are good at. But, no matter our preferred strategies or how well-intentioned we might be, the reality is, none of us are capable of carrying around a toolbox with enough cognitive tools to know what is best in every situation. It's just not possible.

For an example, consider the following. A group of MBAs are going to have a certain set of problem solving tools in common. These tools would be valuable if called upon to forecast the profit to loss ratios for an upcoming product launch. However, this set of *common* tools would limit their ability to consider all the possible variables related to their forecast. In this illustration, the MBAs would likely not know the musical artist management secured to endorse their new product had lyrics in an upcoming album that were going to

---

[5] Page, *The Difference,* 103.

be offensive to a large group of the population consequently reducing product sales by their association with this artist. Perhaps expanding the forecast team beyond those on the accounting team would have helped avoid the public relations debacle in which they were about to be engaged.

For an example closer to home, suppose a group of seminary trained pastors, all of whom have earned their Masters of Divinity degrees, got together to ascertain the best way to enlist volunteers in outreach to the community. Their training predisposes them to a theological perspective. While this perspective and understanding may inspire their actions, it is possible (if not likely) a better way to engage volunteers might be uncovered by including the organizational theory professor at a nearby university or perhaps the volunteer coordinator from a local non-profit in their discussion.

Diverse perspectives enable better solutions to complex problems. C.S. Lewis perhaps summed up the benefits associated with a diverse group of problem solvers best when he said: "Two heads are better than one, not because either is infallible, but because they are unlikely to go wrong in the same direction."[6]

One of the more recognizable examples of crowdsourcing is Wikipedia. While it would be natural to assume the anarchy of the Internet would negate any confidence one might place in the accuracy of the articles on Wikipedia, research conducted by Nature magazine shows the error rate of Wikipedia is actually comparable to that of the Encyclopedia Britannica with only 3.86 errors per article on Wikipedia compared with 2.92 errors per article for Britannica.[7] The key to Wikipedia's success hinges on the fact that those most

---

[6] C. S. Lewis, *God in the Dock: Essays On Theology and Ethics* (Grand Rapids, MI: Eerdmans Pub Co, 1994), 202.
[7] http://news.cnet.com/2100-1038_3-5997332.html

qualified tend to edit and correct the postings of those who are not in an ongoing, albeit somewhat chaotic process.

Now lets look at a few examples of how the business world is attempting to monetize crowdsourcing.

- Innocentive[8] provides a crowdsourcing platform upon which organizations post challenges offering a financial reward to the person or persons who propose the best solution. The amounts of the financial rewards vary from challenge to challenge. For example: Maintaining Crunchy in a Moist Environment - $40,000, Sorting and Compacting of Washroom Waste Bins - $25,000, or Harvesting the Energy in Buildings - $15,000.[9]

- Threadless.com sells t-shirts, however, Threadless.com maintains no t-shirt designers on staff. Instead, their t-shirt designs are submitted by the crowd and selected for production by the crowd who votes on their favorite designs. The crowd submits, the crowd votes, and the crowd affirms their decision by purchasing t-shirts.

- Quirky.com is another example of innovation being fueled by crowdsourcing in that Quirky encourages inventors to submit designs or suggestions for new products to their website. When these ideas are submitted, Quirky encourages people to vote on their favorites and/or contribute ideas for improvement. Quirky then takes the best ideas (those with the greatest number of votes), manufactures them, and brings them to market. A device currently offered for sale on Quirky.com is something called the Pivot Power. Quirky states the inventor thus far has earned over $11,000 while the community of

---

[8] www.innocentive.com
[9] https://www.innocentive.com/ar/challenge/browse

contributors who helped in the design have earned over $18,000. The math would suggest, crowdsourcing works quite well for Quirky.com.

This is all well and good for big business, but what about smaller groups or organizations that are unable to design and build their own crowdsourcing platforms: Ideascale[10] to the rescue. Ideascale enables the creation of custom crowdsourcing platforms to meet the needs of a variety of organizations both large and small. In the large category, the Department of Energy is using this platform to help uncover "green" solutions to the energy challenges facing us in what they are calling their Energy Challenge.[11] On the smaller end of the spectrum, Ideascale is the platform used for Crowdsourcing Theology projects.

These are just a few examples that help make clear how crowdsourcing is being used in product development or research initiatives. But, what about the theological appropriateness of using crowdsourcing to help solve some of the difficult challenges facing our Church? The best way to answer this question was to conduct a crowdsourcing experiment to find out. This book is the result of just such an experiment.

Here is the invitation[12] that announced and invited people to participate in this theological crowdsourcing experiment via social media.

"Christianity is a body clothed in words. However, our garb has become garbled and our apparel is no longer apparent. Christianity seems lost for words because it is lost in words. It is when any words will do that words have to be chosen most carefully. It is time to address our identity crisis and identify those words that make us who we are.

---

[10] http://www.ideascale.com
[11] http://energychallenge.energy.gov
[12] http://www.crowdsourcingtheology.com/crowdsourcing_theology/100_Words.html

What are the words that bridge the centuries, the words that chime on every page of church history? What are the most beautiful words in the Christian vocabulary? What are the words by which we live, the words over which we wrangle--our trigger words? In the rank of words time has tried and found true, what are the words that are up high? Or as the Welsh poet and novelist Robert Minhinnick puts it, what are you captured by---what are "the words that haunt, the words that teach,/the words that must overreach" (King Driftwood). What are the 100 words that make us Christian?"[13]

This invitation launched a crowdsourcing theology experiment in which 229 individuals participated, 175 words were submitted, and 1025 votes cast over a research period of 4 months. The contributions were thoughtful, insightful, and inspirational. It is from this fertile soil, The Book of Signs was birthed.

---

[13] Leonard Sweet for this project.

Introduction

We live in a world of signs. There are natural signs humanity has observed since the beginning of time and there are less than natural signs of our own creation. In fact, life as we know it would be next to impossible without these signs.

In the world of semiotics, a sign is anything that has meaning. Individual letters, words, images, sounds, smells, and tastes are all signs, as are a smile, a kiss, a hug, or a tear.

Identity is made visible through a rather elaborate system of signs: clothes, hair, language, demeanor, and even selfies (#justbeingmyself) are ways we announce to the world who we are and what we consider important. Even our skin is being used for sign space as we ink permanent images onto ourselves that make visible the story of our lives.

In the not too distant past for many of us (and currently in certain parts of the world) one's survival depended upon the ability to read signs to track one's dinner. The signs at the center of the trackers attention might be footprints in the mud or snow, or perhaps animal "droppings, or scat, remains of food, claw marks on trees or shrubs, and trails or corridors through the forest, as well as some not-so-obvious signs, such as turned stones and stunted vegetation."[14] The tracker's ability to read these signs tell them where the animal has been, what it has been doing, where it is going, and more importantly what animal they are following.

---

[14] Paul Rezendes, *Tracking and the Art of Seeing: How to Read Animal Tracks and Sign*, 2nd ed. (New York: HarperCollins, 1999), 24.

While most of us today are not scanning the savannah in search of sustenance, we are however quite adept at traversing the economic terrain in search of those items that might satisfy our culinary quest. Evolutionary Biologist Carol Yoon suggests our ancient tracking skills have simply been re-purposed for the new environment in which we now find ourselves.[15] In essence, we are still hunter-gatherers, we are just no longer tracking animals in their natural habitat but instead are maneuvering our way to aisle 7 in our preferred grocery garden.

Sign Reading Tools

The primary tools we use in the reading of signs in life, the forest, or the marketplace are the same: sight, sound, smell, taste, touch, and when these are combined with time, we can add experience.

Vision

Vision is one of the primary tools in our sign reading toolbox. It locates us within our environment. It enables us to see where we have been, to see where we are, and in a sense, vision allows us to look into the future as we peer in the direction of our destination. This directionality of vision has a drawback though: we can only see in the direction we are pointed.

Hearing

Hearing is omni-directional in that we can hear a full 360 degrees irrespective of which direction we are facing. Hearing can alert us to the presence of a friend or foe as it helps us locate the source of a sound. Hearing

---

[15] Carol Kaesuk Yoon, *Naming Nature: The Clash between Instinct and Science* (New York: W.W. Norton, ©2009), 280.

also rises to the top of our sensory hierarchy at night, as darkness does not obscure our ability to hear.

Smell

We can see and hear things at great distance, but smell is more intimate. Smell exists at the point where the outside enters in. Even though the odor may originate far away, this sense informs us of an invisible presence and alerts our eyes and ears to search for its source.

Taste

Taste is unique in the senses in that what we taste not only enters in, it becomes part of us. Taste can alert us when something should not be eaten and taste can drive us to pursue something we have a taste for. As such, taste is the most intimate of senses.

Touch

Touch implies a closeness and familiarity. To feel the warmth or the texture one must be near enough to touch. Touch can be used to explore or touch can be used to push away. But touch also goes beyond the physical in that when a story or a scene or a person affects us in certain ways we say that we are touched...touched in ways that make little sense to our senses.

Experience

Vision, hearing, smell, taste, and touch are the tools in our semiotic toolbox, but we learn to use these tools through experience.

We have seen this before.

We have heard this before.

We have smelled this before.

We have tasted this before.

We have felt this before.

All of these experiences combine in ways that enable us to successfully make our way in this world, but they also leave marks of their own. These markings reveal where we have been, what we have been doing, where we are going, and more importantly who we are. We are the sum of these experiences even when these experiences don't seem to add up.

Jesus Signs

Jesus was a man of many signs...signs that were rich in meaning.

But so that you may know that the Son of Man has authority on earth to forgive sins"—he said to the paralytic—"I say to you, stand up, take your mat and go to your home."[16]

As the news of Jesus and the signs he was performing began to circulate, John the Baptist sent two of his disciples to find Jesus and ask him a question: *"Are you the one who is to come, or are we to wait for another"? Jesus answered them. "Go and tell John what you have seen and heard: the blind receive their sight, the lame walk, the lepers are cleansed, the deaf hear, the dead are raised, the poor have good news brought to them."*[17]

Did Jesus answer John's question by discussing his pedigree or the many ways in which prophecy aligned with his existence and presence? No, Jesus pointed to the signs...signs that revealed who Jesus was and the truth of his identity.

---

[16] Matthew 9:6, Mark 2:10-11, Luke 5:24

Today, the majority of the signs we utilize to validate our identity as followers of Jesus are found in things we can count. For churches, these signs typically revolve around the following:

How many people are in your congregation?

How many baptisms did you have last year?

How many new members have joined?

What percentage of members tithe?

As individuals, we tend to have a different set of metrics to determine the depth of our discipleship:

How often do you attend church?

How often do you read your bible?

Been on any mission trips lately?

Are you a tither?

We love to count because counting is verifiable and measurable, but we should count the cost of this strategy since it places the accountant at the head of the table rather than Jesus.[18]

So, if Jesus' answer to the question from John's disciples concerning whether Jesus was the Messiah or not was revealed by the God signs in Jesus' life, what are the God signs in our lives and the life of our churches that reveal the truth of our identity as followers of Jesus? The Book of Signs is an attempt

---

[17] Luke 7:22, Matthew 11:3-5
[18] Thanks to Peter Block and his book The Answer to How is Yes for this insight.

to answer that question as it provides us with Jesus signs that make sense to our senses.

Each section features a primary word (or sign) contributed by trackers (followers) of Jesus based upon their experience: the sights they have seen, sounds they have heard, scents they have followed, tastes they have learned, feelings they have had, and experiences they have lived—all signs providing evidence that Jesus, the one they were "tracking," was near.

As an author, my task has been to honor the result of their collective wisdom, exploring and expanding upon these signs as a way to help Jesus trackers better recognize the sights, sounds, scents, tastes, feelings, and experiences in their lives that not only keep them on the trail, but reveal a Jesus that is making Himself known in our midst.

Reading the signs of others may bring certain signs you have experienced to mind that are not recorded in this Book of Signs. If it does, there are several pages at the back of the book where you can record signs of your own in the Field Notes section.

And so, this is a handbook or field manual, a book of signs that echo John's question and Jesus' answer: Are you the one, one of the followers of Jesus and is your church a community full of signs pointing to a Jesus that is alive, healthy, and nearby?

Welcome to The Book of Signs.

1 - Hear

Most of us have likely heard at some point we have two ears and one mouth so we will listen more than we talk. While there is some degree of truth in this statement, from a biological perspective, we have two ears for a much more practical purpose: sound localization. As sound arrives at each ear in differing intensities and with delayed arrival times, we are able to quite accurately locate its source. Knowing the source of what we are hearing and who we are listening to can make a big difference... sometimes the difference between life and death.

We find an example of such magnitude in the way sound recognition enables generation after generation of Emperor penguins to survive in the harsh conditions of Antarctica. Each year, after the female penguin lays her single egg, she passes this egg off to her spouse while she and the other girls venture off in search of the open waters and food. This journey may take her up to 50 miles away and separate her from her family for possibly two months. Upon her return, she must locate her somewhat malnourished mate who has been shielding and caring for their chick during the brutal winter of Antarctica. Research has shown these pairs of penguins locate one another using a two-part sound-producing organ known as the syrinx.[19] To better understand how this organ contributes to spousal localization, scientists conducted tests in which they recorded the voice of a penguin's spouse and played it for their mate to confirm they would respond to this voice...they did. However when the recording was modified in even the slightest manner, the mate did not

---

[19] T Aubin, P Jouventin, and P Hildebrand, "Penguins Use the Two-Voice System to Recognize Each Other." *Proceedings of the Royal Society B: Biological Sciences* 267 (2000): 1081-87, accessed January 22, 2015, http://www.ncbi.nlm.nih.gov/pmc/articles/PMC1690651/.

respond.[20] The familiarity the penguin parents have with the sound of one another's voice enables them to single out and identify each other from perhaps 100,000 competing voices.

As it turns out, people are not that different from emperor penguins in their ability to zero in on the voice of a spouse. In research conducted by Ingrid Johnsrude, she found that when the voice of a spouse is recorded and played back while also playing back a competing, yet unfamiliar voice, the listening spouse was much more accurate when asked to repeat what it was their spouse was saying in this exercise.[21] She discovered the benefit of familiarity was sizable and comparable to the benefit associated with trying to distinguish between sounds emanating from different locations.[22] Interestingly, when playing out the opposite scenario, spouses were also better able to ignore the familiar voice of their spouse to listen to an unfamiliar voice as compared with trying to distinguish between two unfamiliar voices.[23] Whether human or emperor penguin, familiarity seems to enhance our ability to hear the voice of those most important to us.

Life in contemporary culture exposes us to an abundance of voices attempting to tell us that completeness, fulfillment, or happiness is found in whatever it is they are selling. Long term exposure to this noise can diminish our ability to discern the voice of Jesus who speaks in contrast to these illusions as he tells us true completeness, fulfillment, or happiness can only be found in him.

---

[20] Ibid.
[21] http://www.psychologicalscience.org/index.php/news/releases/your-spouses-voice-is-easier-to-hear-and-easier-to-ignore.html
[22] Ibid.
[23] Ibid.

However, just as a pair of emperor penguins can hear the voice of their mate from amongst the cacophony of competing voices and a spouse can zero in on the voice of their beloved, we as the Body of Christ, the bride of a most holy groom, must be intimately familiar with the voice of Jesus if we are to successfully follow him today.

The ability to recognize his voice above all others, both inside and outside the walls of the church, is a sign the footsteps you are following, are the footsteps of Jesus.

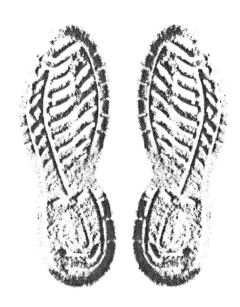

2 - Grace

Anyone who has ever been truly lost knows the vulnerability and despair associated with this experience. The kind of lost we are talking about here is not the lost we get while driving, for this kind of lost can easily be overcome by asking for directions or consulting the GPS.

The lostness to which we refer is more like being lost on a raft in the ocean with dwindling supplies, not knowing which way to go or having the strength to move that direction if we could. If we were to find ourselves in the midst of this kind of lostness, a lostness where the hopelessness of the situation threatened to overtake us, then the joy of being found could not be overstated.

John Newton wrote a song about being lost and then found we know as Amazing Grace.

Amazing Grace, how sweet the sound,

That saved a wretch like me.

I once was lost but now am found,

Was blind, but now I see.

This anthem of human redemption tells the story of being spiritually lost in ones wretchedness and blind to the God that stands before us, but then celebrates the joy of being found and rescued through the grace of God...Amazing Grace.

Interesting, one is not found unless a search is in progress, for if one somehow makes their way back to familiar surroundings, they were not found, they simply found their way home. This distinction is critical in our understanding of Christianity in that Christians are those who have been found and rescued from the wretchedness of their situation, not those who found their way to some spiritual destination. Being found implies a finder and it is in the presence of this finder…Jesus…that we are found in grace.

And so, if we are to look for signs that we are following Jesus, we should look for evidence of grace in our lives. Are we graceful with the graceless, hopeful with the hopeless, helpful with the helpless, and merciful with the merciless? These signs of grace will signify that Jesus is near and the footsteps we are following will lead us home.

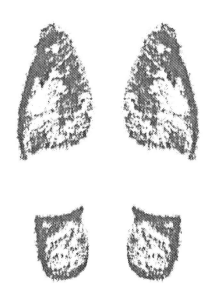

3 - Love

If we perform a Google search for the word "love", we find almost 3 billion results. Search love in film...1 billion, love in music... 1.73 billion, love in books... 1.1 billion etc. Searching for love on Google or any other search engine is quite simple. However, in life that search can be more difficult as even defining love proves somewhat problematic. We love what we do and yet we love a day off. We love our family, we love our spouse, we love our children, we love our friends, but we also love chocolate, fashion, fast cars, and anything on sale.

Even the terminology we associate with finding love indicates that our search was not necessarily intentional, we simply fell in love. Some seem to be somewhat gravitationally challenged as they fall in and out of love at the drop of a hat, while others, perhaps more sure of their footing never seem to stumble into love. And yet, our search for love continues.

We have learned about love from those who have gone before us on this journey. They have done their best to provide us with a roadmap to this most intimate of destinations, but the map isn't clearly marked and the signs are easy to overlook.

And so, our search for love takes us down many roads. Some roads turn out to be dead ends. Some roads seem promising but prove only to be detours. Still others lead us in the right direction as they enable us to see love a little clearer, but in the end, stop short of our destination.

This search for love is not for the faint of heart. Some grow tired, settling for something else and calling it love. Others attempt to redirect their energies toward a less elusive endeavor in hopes that success, power, or prestige will quench the fire, but in the end, love's embers remain un-fanned.

The best example of love for this book of signs can be found in what is likely the most familiar text in the Bible.

"For God so loved the world, that he gave his only begotten Son, that whosoever believeth in him should not perish, but have everlasting life."[24]

This kind of love is more than a love we might have for chocolate, fashion, or fast cars. This kind of love requires a sacrifice of that which is nearest and dearest, a re-ordering and restructuring of our lives in Jesus' direction. Finding ourselves in the presence of this kind of love is not the result of a stumble or a fall, it is found in surrender.

And so, if we are to be successful in our search for love, we must pay attention to the signs and consider the evidence that reveals the true nature of the love standing before us. Is it a love similar to the love one has for chocolate, treated as a guilty pleasure only to be enjoyed on special occasions or with great remorse? Is it a love similar to a love of fashion, showing greatest enthusiasm for the novel and new, tiring of love when it shows signs of wear or stress as it can easily be replaced with something new. Or, is it a Jesus kind of love, a love found in surrender, a love without end?

Jesus is the longitude and latitude of this love. No matter our wrong turns, missed turns, or the quantity of our re-turns, our spiritual GPS (God Positioning System) will always recalculate our trajectory, pointing us in the direction that leads to the foot of the cross, for it is there and only there we truly find the meaning of love.

---

[24] John 3:16 KJV

4 - Jesus

It used to be when we referred to someone as a *friend* the implication was that we knew this person, we had spent time with them, knew some of their likes, their dislikes, and maybe even knew their family. However, Facebook has changed the way in which we understand what it means to be a *friend*.

Twitter identifies its connections a little differently and perhaps more accurately, in that the Twitterverse is made up of followers; you follow people and others follow you; there is no implied friendship in the connection.

Granted, Twitter and Facebook can be platforms on which we discover and build new relationships. I have done this and you probably have as well. But, in many cases, if we were to come face to face with these online friends and followers, we would not know it because our eyes and ears would not alert us to their presence, as we have had no experience with them apart from our online interactions.

Animal trackers know that to successfully follow an animal, they need to know as much as possible about the one they are following. They need to know what it looks like, what it sounds like, its habits, and the environments in which it is likely to be found. The longer a tracker follows an animal the deeper they enter into a relationship with its life and the better prepared they are to know where to look for it and when.[25] Without this kind of knowing, the tracker is not following a trail, they are merely out on a walk.

Success in our attempts to follow Jesus will be determined by the kind of following we are doing. Are we following Jesus in the same way we typically

---

[25] Rezendes, *Tracking and the Art of Seeing,* 15.

follow people on the Internet…disconnected and distant…unable to recognize Jesus if he stood before us?

Or, will we know him when we see him and recognize the sound of his voice when we hear it because we have spent time with him, know his likes and dislikes, know his habits and the habitats where he can be found, and maybe even know some of the members of his crazy family.

Knowing Jesus in the way one truly knows a friend is a sign the tracks we are following lead in his direction.

5 - Bless

In contemporary church culture, we are not only dressed for success, we are seemingly blessed for success. We say we are blessed when we get a job or a promotion. We say we are blessed when we have good health or are cured from some malady. We even go so far as to say we are blessed when our favorite team wins or we get a good parking spot close to the door of the movie theater. Being blessed has come to mean success, health, money, friends, new cars, and new clothes as blessing is increasingly evidenced through abundance and good fortune.

Ancient Israel's understanding of being blessed was not that different from ours today as they too felt being rich, eating well, drinking well, or being entertained were the rewards and evidence of a blessed life.[26] However, a life spent pursuing these types of blessings commits us to a path where we can never truly be happy as the quest for just a little bit more becomes the unattainable trajectory our journey.

Jesus, rather than allow his disciples to pursue this path without end, provided instead, a set of coordinates where true blessing is to be found in what we call the Sermon on the Mount. The sermon begins:

"Blessed are the poor in spirit, for theirs is the kingdom of heaven.

Blessed are those who mourn, for they will be comforted."[27]

When we read these words, it is easy for us to interpret them as being directed toward someone else, someone in the midst of a difficult time in their

---

[26] Matthew Henry. *Commentary of the Whole Bible.* (Grands Rapids: Zondervan, 1960), 1219.

24

lives...words of encouragement if you will. However, Jesus was not attempting to encourage the less fortunate or provide a theological salve for those wishing to embrace their privileged position in life with clear conscience. Jesus was instead redefining, revolutionizing, and redrawing the map to the place where his followers can truly experience what it means to be blessed.

If Jesus meant what he said and this where we will truly find blessings, then how can those of us who are firmly planted in the rich soil of abundance, uproot ourselves and embark on this journey? Must we give away our resources and pursue a life of misery? No, but the path of Jesus does reveal a different set of signs.

In his re-framing of what it means to be blessed Jesus tells us we must not look to transitory moments of abundance as evidence of blessing because these seasons will pass as the fruits of our labors fail to satisfy.

Instead, we will find ourselves being blessed when we enter into the misery and walk alongside those who are beaten down and exhausted from their experience of life. This is where Jesus calls us to join him and this is where we will experience what it means to be blessed.

---

[27] Matthew 5:3-4

6 - Mystery

The format of a mystery is fairly predictable, as it doesn't stray far from a familiar formula; something unexpected happens, witnesses are interviewed, evidence is examined, and the mystery is solved. Good mysteries, of course, come with a quantity of twists and turns, but ultimately, the guilty are revealed and suffer the consequences of their actions.

This is how a mystery works. This is how they are supposed to work. This is how they always work...well, most of the time.

One fateful day, Pilate was confronted with a mystery. Before him stood a man accused of crimes he did not commit; accused of blasphemy toward both God and Caesar among other things. Pilate interrogated those who claimed to be witnesses. He tried his best to understand the circumstances. He even questioned Jesus to see what kind of a defense he would put forth. But Jesus offered no defense, no excuse, no reason to deny the crowd the verdict and judgment they were demanding. This was, no doubt, a mystery to Pilate since even the guilty tend to proclaim their innocence. But, an innocent man offering no defense, this was indeed a mystery.

Pilate tried to set him free, tried to help the crowd see the folly of their endeavor, but the crowd would have not part of it. So, he gave in to their wishes, sending Jesus off to suffer the punishment for the crimes he did not commit. Ultimately, Jesus remained a mystery to Pilate, as he never became aware that the truth[28] was standing right in front of him the whole time.

---

[28] John 14:6 - *"I am the way, and the truth, and the life."[28] Jesus*

Oftentimes, it is easy for us to approach the mystery of Jesus in ways similar to a crime scene investigator or even Pilate.

We interrogate the testimony of the witnesses. We compare and contrast, looking for confirmation or perhaps contradiction. We search for evidence that might confirm or deny the truth of the story, all the while, completely missing the truth that stands before us.

In the mysteries we are used to, the guilty are condemned while the innocent go free. In Jesus' story, the innocent is condemned while the guilty go free.

Followers of Jesus are the guilty ones, those who have heard the stories, witnessed Jesus presence on the trail, and embraced the freedom found in the truth of life's greatest mystery: the mystery that is Christ himself.

7 - Faith

Monarchs are one of the most recognizable butterflies in North America. We have studied them in elementary school, watched them break free of a cocoon in science class, and hopefully had the privilege to observe them on one of their annual migrations across the United States. These migrations begin in the fall as the monarchs embark on a journey south of up to 3000 miles in search of their traditional wintering sites. While the distance traveled is impressive in its own right, what is even more amazing is they fly to the same location each year, even though the monarchs on this trip have never been there before. Those who begin the journey south in the fall are not the same ones who return home in the spring, as the round-trip migration of the monarch is a multi-generational effort. Apparently monarchs are made for the journey rather than the destination.

The Bible is filled with amazing journeys of faith in which God's people:

...built a life boat on the news of a storm[29]

...walked away from and walked toward[30]

...birthed a nation from tired loins[31]

...left their homes in search of a promised land[32]

...walked through deep waters on dry land[33]

...And much, much more.

----

[29] Hebrews 11:7
[30] Hebrews 11:8-10
[31] Hebrews 11:11-12
[32] Hebrews 11:24-28

In spite of these impressive accomplishments, scripture says: *Not one of these people, even though their lives of faith were exemplary, got their hands on what was promised.*[34]

From the modern western perspective, this doesn't seem fair. It goes against our cultural code of ethics that promises rewards for those sick with it, who work hard. However, in spite of the great accomplishments of God's people on this journey, those who began the migration, never reached their destination; for God's people of faith, like the monarchs, the journey is the destination.

As people of faith we must ask ourselves the following questions. Are we willing to set the destination point of our journey beyond the horizon of our experience or abilities? Are we willing to work toward that which will ultimately remain slightly beyond our reach? Are we willing to play an essential role in the journey, without ever getting our hands on what was promised?

Faith is more than believing for a new job, a new car, a meaningful relationship, or even a healing. Faith is for the journey. Faith is what moves followers on the trail of Jesus forward toward God's vision of the future and it is faith that enables us to remain steadfast on that journey.

What will be our great stories of faith that will be told to those who follow us on our journey home?

---

[33] Hebrews 11:29
[34] Hebrews 11:39 (The Message)

8 - Shalom

When viewing a photo of our planet taken from miles overhead, it's hard not to be struck with a sense of wonder as this beautiful little blue ball floats in an ocean of stars. When presented with this vision it's easy to imagine God viewing creation for the first time and pronouncing, *it is good*. But the reality of life at ground level in our world lies at some distance from this initial assessment, as too many of us are found living in conditions where air is un-breathable, water un-drinkable, and life situations un-livable; living apart from Shalom.

Shalom is a Hebrew word expressing the harmonious state of existence between God and creation. Many of our current conditions reflect not the harmony of creation with God, but the disharmony that resulted when shalom fell victim to temptation.

In many ways, the story of God's people is the story of the journey back to shalom, back to the garden of original intention.

Our return to shalom is not found in the distancing of ourselves from the unfortunate realities of our world. Instead, the path home requires us to become co-creators with God in the establishment of shalom in the midst of our current situation.

Shalom will be found as the people of God breathe life into those gasping for breath, pour living water into the hearts of dry souls, and situate themselves alongside those in unlivable situations.

The journey for followers of Jesus will be anything but peaceful, but we will find ourselves grateful, for the harvest of the garden will prove bountiful as shalom is restored.

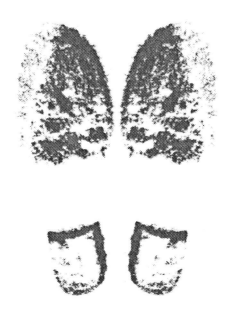

9 - Fellowship

One of the first things Jesus did after embarking on his mission was to invite 12 individuals into fellowship. It was in the midst of this fellowship the disciples learned from Jesus as he not only taught and healed, but also as he walked and talked and gathered the fellowship together for conversation at meal time. It was in the closeness of this fellowship the disciples came to believe Jesus was the Messiah.

Just as the disciples learned from Jesus, they also learned from each other. They learned who was quick tempered, who was self-interested, who was doubtful, and eventually who would betray them, for the betrayal came from one of their own who grew impatient with the trajectory of the fellowship.

After the crucifixion of Jesus, the disciples sought solace and a sense of safety in their fellowship as they tried to make sense of recent events. Their confusion and doubt soon disappeared as Jesus, back from the dead, appeared in their midst. The fellowship was restored. Well, almost restored as Thomas, one of the members of their fellowship was not there for the reunion.

Later, when the others told Thomas they had seen Jesus, that he was alive, Thomas kept the fellowship at arms length stating: *"Unless I see the mark of the nails in his hands, and put my finger in the mark of the nails and my hand in his side, I will not believe."*[35] In other words, he did not trust the testimony of his fellowship.

It is easy to read through this part of the story without pondering why Thomas questioned the statement of his fellow disciples. Thomas knew them. They had all been on the same journey with Jesus. Knowing them as he did,

---

[35] John 20:25

he likely knew they rarely agreed on anything. And yet, here they were, in agreement, telling Thomas they had seen him, that Jesus was alive, and yet, he doubted them.

But maybe it wasn't doubt at all. Maybe Thomas didn't want to be the only disciple who had not seen Jesus, the one whose faith had to depend on the testimony of others in the fellowship. Maybe there was a certain jealousy in Thomas. Maybe he was a little bit angry or disappointed that Jesus chose to reveal himself to the group when Thomas happened to be away doing something else. Maybe Thomas wanted a personal encounter too so that he wouldn't feel like "that" disciple who must not have been important enough for Jesus to wait until they were all together to show himself. We don't know.

But we do know, eight days later, Jesus appeared to the fellowship and directly addressed Thomas: *"Put your finger here and see my hands. Reach out your hand and put it in my side. Do not doubt but believe."*[36] Thomas responded: *"My Lord and my God!"*[37] The fellowship had been restored.

Fellowships are not homogenous groups of people (or at least they shouldn't be if we are to follow Jesus' example.) Fellowships consist of a diverse group of individuals committed to doing their best to follow Jesus together. This is the content of Jesus' fellowship and if we are to be considered followers of Jesus, it should be the make-up or our fellowships as well.

Followers of Jesus celebrate the diversity in the fellowship we have been invited into knowing that when we stumble or loose our footing on the journey, others will be there to lift us up and restore us to the fellowship of believers.

---

[36] John 20:27
[37] John 20:28

And so, to determine if the trail we are following leads to Jesus, look to your left and to your right. If you are alone, the trail is likely not one that leads to Jesus. If you find yourself in the midst of a beautifully varied group of travelers, stay close to one another and enjoy the journey.

Signs that we are following Jesus will be found in the vibrancy of our fellowships.

10 - Scandalous

Scandals seem to populate the news consistently these days. If its not the type of scandal that disrupts lives or destroys careers, its a fashionable kind of scandal, engaged in to bring the someone or something to the forefront of public attention.

But, what about a different kind of scandalous; a scandalous that exists to serve the needs of others or to illuminate the wrongs of the day? We don't hear so much about that kind of scandalous these days, especially not in church, even though the Christian faith was born in scandal.

• Jesus' earthly family tree was populated with prostitutes, adulterers, murderers, and Gentiles.
• He was born to an unmarried couple.
• He was born on the wrong side of the tracks.
• He claimed to be the Son of God.
• He dined with outcasts.
• He fellowshipped with those living on the fringes of society.
• He healed lepers with a touch and blindness with dirt and spit.
• He challenged the religious authorities at every turn.
• He turned the social order upside-down.
• He claimed to have the power to call down angels to come to his defense and rescue… but in the end he accepted his fate and died a merciless death.

The life of Jesus was scandalous in most every cultural way, and yet many of us do our best to avoid scandal, choosing instead to locate ourselves on a path that leads to comfort and security.

If we want to determine the footsteps we are following are the scandalous footsteps of Jesus, we need to ask ourselves a few questions.

- Do we accept the out-laws along with the in-laws in our families?
- Do we embrace and care for those who were conceived or are pregnant apart from marriage or do we stand and judge condescendingly from afar?
- Are we gracious and welcoming to those whose lot in life has landed them on the wrong side of the tracks or do we remain safe and secure in our gated communities?
- Do we openly admit to being followers of Jesus or do we expose our Christian identity only when convenient or in the presence of other Christians?
- Do we open our pantries and engage in table fellowship with those less fortunate or do we store away our resources for ourselves?
- Do we have relationships with those living on the fringe of society or do we walk by with headphones in our ears, hoping to avoid eye contact?
- Are we willing to get our hands dirty in the caring for the untouchable?
- Do we challenge the cultural and religious status quos or do we embrace it to avoid confrontation?
- Are we willing to engage our culture for change rather than retreat to our sanctuaries for safety?
- Are we willing to embrace and live out the scandalous lifestyle of Jesus?

The signs in our lives will give us away. Are we scandalous followers of Jesus, or is the fact that we call ourselves followers of Jesus…scandalous?

11 - Trinity

Even though the word *trinity* or a complete doctrine of the *trinity* is nowhere to be found in the scriptures, the understanding of God manifesting in the Trinitarian model of Father, Son, and Holy Spirit is a well excepted concept within Christianity.

Interestingly, when Jesus chose to clarify his identity for the disciples, he chose to explain himself in a very triune manner: *"I am the way, and the truth, and the life."*[38] He is not just the *way* as an example of proper living; not just a philosophical *truth* to be pursued or debated; and not just an example of a *life* well lived; Jesus is the living sign for those who follow.

In Christianity, we tend to divide ourselves into a variety of camps. There are those of us who think our faith is best expressed through activities that fall under the heading of social justice. And, there are others who feel our primary calling is to preach the Bible to an unbelieving culture. However, a proclamation of the gospel does not ring true apart from the service of others. And, social justice when enacted apart from the truth is not truly just. The first is the way without the truth and the second is the truth without the way. One provides help for today without hope for the future while the other provides hope for the future without help for today[39].

Without the three-fold manifestation of Jesus' followers as people of the *way* and the *truth*, we are a broken body, unable to lead others into a Jesus kind of *life*.

---

[38] John 14:6
[39] Thomas E. Ingram, *The New Normal: a Diagnosis the Church Can Live With*, 1.0 ed. (Tulsa: Linen Publishing, 2014), 125.

Signs that we are following Jesus will be found in our living of the *way* and the *truth* that enable abundant *life*.

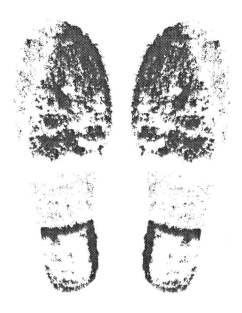

12 - Thirsty

Most of us experience some degree of thirst on a daily basis. We get thirsty because our body requires us to consume a quantity of liquid each day so it can function properly. Research tells us men typically need 13 cups of water per day while women require 9. [40]

A failure on our part to consume the water our bodies require causes a state of dehydration. Mild dehydration can cause a lack of energy, dry skin, or perhaps a headache while severe dehydration can result in extreme thirst, low blood pressure, rapid heartbeat, or unconsciousness.[41] For most of us in Western culture, the solution to this problem is close at hand as water is perhaps our most inexpensive commodity.

There is another kind of thirst, however, a thirst none of us can avoid... a spiritual thirst...a thirst for meaning, a thirst for purpose, and a thirst for love. These thirsts are often the driving forces in our lives as we search for something - anything that will satisfy this thirst, keeping a sense of spiritual dehydration at a distance.

Scientist's tell us at the point we become thirsty, we are already dehydrated. To avoid this dehydration, we are told we should drink water before we become thirsty. This prescription seems to apply to our problem of spiritual dehydration as well. If we maintain adequate quantities of meaning, purpose, and love in our lives, we will be spiritually hydrated and avoid the cravings that cause many of us to walk down destructive paths in search of

---

[40] http://www.mayoclinic.org/healthy-living/nutrition-and-healthy-eating/in-depth/water/art-20044256?pg=1
[41] http://www.mayoclinic.org/diseases-conditions/dehydration/basics/symptoms/con-20030056

that which can satiate our thirst. But how can followers of Jesus achieve this state of spiritual hydration?

One day, Jesus encountered a Samaritan woman seeking water at Jacob's well. As she prepared to draw water from the well, a conversation ensued in which Jesus told her: *"Everyone who drinks of this water will be thirsty again, but those who drink of the water that I will give them will never be thirsty."*[42] The woman responded: *"Sir, give me this water, so that I may never be thirsty or have to keep coming here to draw water."* She mistakenly thought Jesus was talking about the kind of water she came seeking at the well.

Then, in what seems like a rather awkward non-sequitur, Jesus asks the woman to go get her husband, to which the woman replied: *"I have no husband."* [43] Jesus agrees and then clarifies: *"you have had five husbands, and the one you have now is not your husband."*[44]

In this statement, Jesus identified the root of the problem: just as the water in Jacob's well required her to return again and again to satisfy her physical thirst, the quest for meaning, purpose, and love in her life had driven her to bounce from relationship to relationship as those wells had run dry, no longer able to satisfy her spiritual thirst, a thirst that can only be quenched by Jesus.

And so, to determine if the path we are on is leading us in the direction of Jesus, we must discern if we have developed a taste for water from the cultural wells that surround us, water that ultimately will not satisfy. Or, are we quenching our thirst with living waters, waters that spring forth to an eternal life. Our answer will determine if the path we are on leads to Jesus.

---

[42] John 4:13-14
[43] John 4:17
[44] John 4:18

13 - Relationship

Identities don't just happen; they are constructed and revealed in relationship with others.[45] The first and arguably most influential of these identity building relationships is the one we have with those who brought us into this world, for it is our parents who laid the groundwork for who we have become. As we grow, this circle of influence expands to include our extended family, friends, neighbors, classmates, co-workers, bosses, acquaintances, and lets not forget the images and messages that barrage us each day via electronic media attempting to mold us into attentive and loyal consumers.

Somehow in the midst of this mulligan stew of influences an identity emerges. However, to be fair, most of us do not maintain a single identity; we have a variety of identities. Some of these identities are *defined* by fixed relationships: mother, father, son, daughter, sister, or brother. Others are *expressed* through relational action: caretaker, nurturer, provider, teacher, helper, or encourager. Some are *learned* through an educational relationship: surgeon, scientist, lawyer, teacher, or architect. While others are *uncovered* in relationship: gifted, insightful, or thoughtful. And, unfortunately some identities are *thrust* upon us: child abuse victim, accident survivor, divorced, or widowed. Identity is found in a variety of relationships.

The Bible tells the story of our relationship with God. To better understand the nature of this relationship, we must go back to the beginning...literally, for in the beginning God said: *"Let us make humankind in our image, according to our likeness."* [46]

---

[45] James A. Holstein and Jaber F. Gubrium, *The Self We Live By: Narrative Identity in a Postmodern World* (New York: Oxford University Press, USA, 1999), 124.
[46] Genesis 1:26

There is much to learn about our identity in this statement. First, God said "Let us." Us is a plural. It is a statement of the relationship that exists within the Trinity: Father, Son, and Holy Spirit.

Secondly, God said humankind would be made in "our likeness." While likeness most certainly implies a variety of characteristics, we do not have to dig very deep to discern one aspect of that likeness mirrors the relational aspect of our Trinitarian God...identity is found in relationship.

One day the disciples asked Jesus an identity question: "Who is the greatest in the kingdom of heaven?"[47] Jesus replied: "Truly I tell you, unless you change and become like children, you will never enter the kingdom of heaven." There are a variety of interpretations concerning the meaning of this scripture, many of which revolve around power and dependency. However, let us not miss that which is easy to overlook: even though the disciples were asking an identity question (who is the greatest), Jesus answered the question in terms of relationship (how to be great).

Greatness in the kingdom is not found in who we are, but rather in whose we are. We are children of God, children birthed out of relationship and for relationship. It is from this firm foundation that followers of Jesus become who we are truly meant to be.

---

[47] Matthew 18:1

14 - Redeemed

Couponing in the United States is a growing trend with the majority of coupons being issued for what the industry calls consumer packaged goods[48] such as food, beverages, clothing, and cleaning supplies etc. 305 billion of these coupons were issued in 2012 with 2.9 billion of those being redeemed for a total savings on purchases of $3.6 billion dollars.[49] Those that are active couponers know that to take advantage of these savings, they must be redeemed under the rules of the coupon. Here are some of the rules.

- *Manufacturer will redeem coupon in accordance with terms of the redemption policy.*

- *Not valid in combination with other offers.*

- *Limit one coupon per transaction.*

- *Coupon may not be bought, reproduced, transferred, or sold.*

- *Must be redeemed before expiration date.*

Failure to redeem the coupon under the rules and conditions set forth by the manufacturer invalidates the coupon.

Ironically, some of us gladly accept the rules associated with coupon redemption while balking at the terms of human redemption. We feel that if we are just a good person or do good things in life, that will be enough for God to redeem us in the end. However, in life, as in coupons, there are rules or criteria for our redemption.

---

[48] http://www.statista.com/topics/1156/coupon-market-trends-in-the-united-states/
[49] http://www.statista.com/topics/1156/coupon-market-trends-in-the-united-states/

- *Manufacturer will redeem coupon in accordance with terms of the redemption policy.*

God has a redemption policy. It centers on Jesus and is only valid when we center our lives on him.

- *Not valid in combination with other offers.*

There is one single offer of redemption through Jesus. Nothing can be added to or taken away from it.

- *Limit one per transaction.*

Our redemption is a one-time event. There is no need for repetitive redeeming.

- *Coupon may not be bought, reproduced, transferred, or sold.*

Our redemption is an individual event. We cannot buy it (as Martin Luther pointed out), reproduce it, transfer it, or sell it to someone else.

- *Expiration date.*

For all practical purposes, we do need to make claim on our redemption before our expiration date.

God is our manufacture and determines the terms of our redemption. Jesus is the redeemer and it is only through him that followers on the trail of Jesus find themselves redeemed in accordance with God's criteria for redemption.

15 - Christ

The story of Jesus is the story of Christ. Or perhaps more accurately, it is the story of the revealing of Jesus as the Christ. The word Christ comes from the Greek word meaning *anointed*. So, when we refer to Jesus as Jesus Christ, or Jesus the Christ, we are acknowledging and proclaiming Jesus as the Messiah, the *anointed* one of God.

Jesus cautioned the disciples to be on the lookout for false christs.

"For false christs and false prophets will rise and show great signs and wonders to deceive, if possible, even the elect."[50]

The Message phrases it a little differently.

"Fake Messiahs and lying preachers are going to pop up everywhere. Their impressive credentials and dazzling performances will pull the wool over the eyes of even those who ought to know better."[51]

When many of us pause to consider these false christs we likely visualize end-time scenarios found in the book of Revelation. However, the reality is, these false christs may be closer than we think.

• When we follow a principle rather than the person of Jesus, we settle for a false Christ.

• When we follow a defender of the poor rather than Jesus, we settle for a false Christ.

---

[50] Matthew 24:24 (NKJV)
[51] Matthew 24:24 (The Message)

• When we follow a provider of justice rather than Jesus, we settle for a false Christ.

This is not to diminish these actions, they are good, but they are actions and not a person capable of being followed.

• Jesus was not the Christ because his ideas or teachings were worthy of imitation.

• Jesus was not the Christ because he was a defender of the poor.

• Jesus was not the Christ because he was a provider of justice.

Jesus was the Christ because he was the anointed one, the Messiah, the Son of God.

In 1964, Dr. Milton Rokeach published a book titled *The Three Christs of Ypsilanti*. The book chronicles the story of Dr. Rokeach's experiment in which he brought together three delusional psychiatric patients who claimed the same identity, that of Jesus Christ.[52] In an afterward to the book written some 20 years later, Dr. Rokeach stated that "while I had failed to cure the three Christs of their delusions, they had succeeded in curing me of mine - of my God-like delusion that I could change them by omnipotently and omnisciently arranging and rearranging their daily lives."[53] Bertrand Russell perhaps sums up Rokeach's revelation best: "Every man would like to be God, if it were possible; some few find it difficult to admit the impossibility."[54]

---

[52] Milton Rokeach, *The Three Christs of Ypsilanti* (New York: NYRB Classics, 2011), location 851, Kindle ebook.
[53] Ibid., location 6731.
[54] Bertrand Russell, *RC Series Bundle: Power: A New Social Analysis (Routledge Classics)* (New York: Routledge, 2004), 3.

Like Rokeach's admission, something in us wants to be the savior, wants to fix the situation, to make everything better. But when we self-anoint ourselves as the solution, we take on a role that was never meant for us; we become false christs.

As followers of Jesus, we must learn to live and act like Jesus, but in doing so, we must not elevate ourselves or our cause above the person of Christ, for our cause is a cause above all other causes: to be a disciple, a follower of the anointed one: Jesus, the one true Christ.

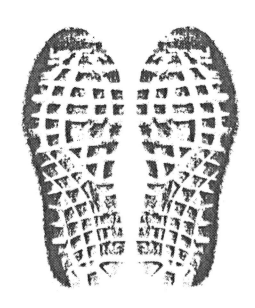

16 - Irreligious

How can being irreligious be a sign we are following Jesus? The answer hinges on our definition of what it means to be religious. According to Funk & Wagnall's, being *religious* means, "feeling and manifesting religion"[55] with religion being defined as "any system of faith and worship."[56] By these definitions we can conclude we are religious when we manifest a system of faith and worship.

No doubt, the Pharisees in Jesus' time considered themselves religious, and yet when Jesus appeared claiming to be the fulfillment of their messianic prophesies, they rejected him, ultimately orchestrating his execution. Jesus even told them he did not come to abolish their religion but instead to fulfill it.[57] And yet, the message and actions of Jesus seemed to infuriate the religious Pharisees. What was it about Jesus that inspired such a negative reaction from those most "religious?"

The opposition to Jesus from the *religious ones* was at least partly fueled by the way in which Jesus tended embarrass them in public with their behavioral and theological inconsistencies. Matthew 23 illustrates this with some of Jesus' most critical polemic of the Pharisees.

"The religion scholars and Pharisees are competent teachers in God's Law. You won't go wrong in following their teachings on Moses. But be careful about following them. They talk a good line, but they don't live it. They don't

---

[55] *Funk and Wagnalls New Comprehensive International Dictionary of the English Language.*, Deluxe reference ed. (Newark, N.J.: Ferguson Pub, 1982), 1064.
[56] Ibid.
[57] Matthew 5:17

take it into their hearts and live it out in their behavior. It's all spit-and-polish veneer.""[58]

So much for tiptoeing around the issue. Jesus continues:

"Instead of giving you God's Law as food and drink by which you can banquet on God, they package it in bundles of rules, loading you down like pack animals. They seem to take pleasure in watching you stagger under these loads, and wouldn't think of lifting a finger to help. Their lives are perpetual fashion shows, embroidered prayer shawls one day and flowery prayers the next."[59]

It's not very difficult to see how the religious leaders might take offense to this, but Jesus doesn't stop there.

"I've had it with you! You're hopeless, you religion scholars, you Pharisees! Frauds! Your lives are roadblocks to God's kingdom. You refuse to enter, and won't let anyone else in either. You're hopeless, you religion scholars and Pharisees! Frauds! You go halfway around the world to make a convert, but once you get him you make him into a replica of yourselves, double-damned."[60]

The Pharisees were indeed religious, very religious, religious about their religion, which brings us to a second definition of the term religious: "strict in performance, conscientious: a religious loyalty."[61] We can be religious about a great many things and engage in them religiously. Some of us exercise

---

[58] Matthew 23:2-3 (The Message)
[59] Matthew 23:4-5 (The Message)
[60] Matthew 23:13-14 (The Message)
[61] Funk and Wagnalls New Comprehensive International Dictionary of the English Language, 1064.

religiously. Some of us adhere to a strict daily schedule religiously, while others count the calories of each meal religiously.

Doing things religiously can give us a sense of security and comfort. But, religiously adhering to a practice or set of practices is more about control...it is about us...it is about what *we* can do. It identifies ourselves as the central character in our life drama; in control of our health, in control of our schedules, in control of our diets, and for those religious about their religion; seemingly in control of our salvation.

Jesus did not come to make religious people. Jesus came to free us from religious bondage through relationship, a relationship that requires us to abandon many of our religious endeavors...in other words...to become irreligious.

17 - Forgiveness

One day, as Jesus was speaking in a crowded room which could hold no one else, some people arrived carrying a paralyzed man. When they could not work their way through the crowd to get the man to Jesus, they went up to the roof and removed a portion so they could lower the man into the room. Just like we would do…right?

When Jesus saw the man and *"saw their faith, he said, "Friend, your sins are forgiven you.""* [62] This of course, angered the religious authorities who were present:" *"Who is this who is speaking blasphemies? Who can forgive sins but God alone?"* [63] Jesus responded to their concerns:" *Which is easier, to say, "Your sins are forgiven you,' or to say, "Stand up and walk'? But so that you may know that the Son of Man has authority on earth to forgive sins"—he said to the one who was paralyzed—"I say to you, stand up and take your bed and go to your home." Immediately he stood up before them, took what he had been lying on, and went to his home, glorifying God."* [64]

This story has typically been highlighted as a way to illuminate the deity of Jesus or perhaps encourage us to pursue Jesus irrespective of the obstacles that lie before us. But, there is something curious in this story that is often overlooked. When Jesus saw the man lying on the mat paralyzed…in obvious need of healing…why did Jesus seemingly overlook the obvious physical condition of the man and instead make a point of forgiving his sins? Did Jesus do this simply to get under the skin of the Pharisees in the room? If this was his intent, it worked.

---

[62] Luke 5:20
[63] Luke 5:21
[64] Luke 5:23-25

Or, was Jesus making a point? Was Jesus announcing to the room that forgiveness of sin was of much greater importance in the life of this man (and likely ours) than physical healing? After all, Jesus only healed the man of his paralysis later as a way to underscore his authority to forgive sins... seemingly an afterthought.

Stories in the Bible are like multi-dimensional trail markers containing several layers of meaning; so let's peel back the layers a bit in hopes of uncovering a deeper understanding.

Why was the man paralyzed? The story does not say.

Was he born this way, paralyzed from birth? Was his condition the result of his own actions or the actions of someone else? Did he come before Jesus willingly or was he brought there against his will?

Or, perhaps more importantly...was his paralysis metaphorical?

Was the man's paralyzed state the result of an inability to either forgive or accept forgiveness? Had he been clinging so tightly to un-forgiveness over something he had done or something done to him that he was now anchored to that event, tethered to that place and time, unable to move forward with his life...paralyzed?

When reading the story of Jesus and the paralytic from the perspective of forgiveness, we must ask ourselves a question: are we being held captive or are we holding others captive, paralyzed in a cage of un-forgiveness?

If we are, we must accept the forgiveness Jesus offers and offer that forgiveness to those who have wronged us so we too will be released from the paralyzing cage of un-forgiveness. It is when we view others and ourselves through a lens of forgiveness that we are better able to rise up from what holds us captive and return to the trail glorifying God.

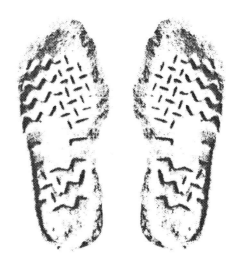

18 - Reconciliation

The Bible is a story of reconciliation or perhaps, more accurately, many stories of reconciliation. One of the most poignant of those stories involves Peter and Jesus.

On the eve of his betrayal, Jesus led the disciples to the Mount of Olives. It is here Jesus told them that during the course of the events to come, all of them would abandon him.[65] Peter, of course, denied that possibility.[66] Jesus turns up the heat by telling Peter, *"this very night, before the cock crows twice, you will deny me three times."*[67] Peter then ups the ante of his denial saying he would rather die than deny Jesus.[68]

A few hours later, Jesus' prophecy came true.

Most of us are familiar with this story, but there is a sub-text to this story we might overlook. Peter and the others had been with Jesus for three years. They had worked alongside him. They had seen the amazing things he had done. They had come to believe Jesus was the Messiah, the Christ, the living incarnation of God in the flesh, and yet, in this instance, they told Jesus he was wrong.

Why this sudden amnesia of their recent history together? How could Peter and the disciples believe all these things about Jesus and then reject his assessment of their future? It doesn't seem to make sense; unless of course we make it personal.

---

[65] Mark 14:27
[66] Mark 14:29
[67] Mark 14:30-31
[68] Mark 14:30-31

Jesus makes clear his assessment of our human condition: we are broken people in a broken world and unless we follow him, our path leads us to destruction. But, so often, our response is like that of the disciples...even Peter. We say that's not true, that we can handle it, that we are the masters of our universe, that Jesus is wrong...about us.

Peter's bravado was short lived that night, for it was not long before Jesus was seized and taken before the high priest Caiaphas. Peter followed Jesus "at a distance".[69]

Later, while Peter was warming himself from the cold by a fire, he was asked about his relationship with Jesus and, as predicted, each time he was asked, Peter denied even knowing Jesus.[70] When Peter realized it had happened just as Jesus had said, we are told Peter "went out and cried and cried and cried."[71]

I bet he did.

It's hard to imagine the depth of anguish Peter must have felt at that moment. If you remember, Peter was the disciple who when questioned directly by Jesus over his identity had responded: "You are the Messiah, the Son of the living God."[72] This very night he had even vowed to die with Jesus rather than deny him. And yet, when confronted and challenged by a servant girl...a servant girl, Peter caved, he folded, he denied even knowing Jesus.

Fortunately for Peter, this was not the end of the story.

---

[69] Mark 14:54
[70] Matthew 26:59-75
[71] Matthew 26:59-75
[72] Matthew 16:16

After the resurrection, Jesus appeared to the disciples on the beach while they were out fishing. They came to shore and joined Jesus for breakfast. When breakfast concluded, it was reconciliation time.

"After breakfast, Jesus said to Simon Peter, "Simon, son of John, do you love me more than these?" "Yes, Master, you know I love you." Jesus said, "Feed my lambs." He then asked a second time, "Simon, son of John, do you love me?" "Yes, Master, you know I love you." Jesus said, "Shepherd my sheep." Then he said it a third time: "Simon, son of John, do you love me?" Peter was upset that he asked for the third time, "Do you love me?" so he answered, "Master, you know everything there is to know. You've got to know that I love you.""[73]

With each of these confessions, Peter's burden of guilt and shame must have lightened. It is a powerful moment. But, the ultimate confession lies in Peter's third response: *"Master, you know everything there is to know."*[74]

Earlier at the Mount of Olives, when Jesus told Peter what would happen... Peter's denial of Jesus... Peter balked and told Jesus he did not know what he was talking about. Peter's last confession was his admission that yes, Jesus, you know everything there is to know, and yet you still love me. Peter was reconciled to Jesus.

Jesus pursued Peter to reconcile their relationship just as Jesus pursues reconciliation with us today. He does this in spite of our failures, our shortcomings, and even our rejections of him in the past. Whatever we have done or said or thought about him, Jesus pursues us to shorten the distance of the pathway back to him.

---

[73] John 21:15-17 The Message
[74] Ibid.

Jesus followers are those who have walked the path to reconciliation, who do not keep Jesus at a distance, and who work to reconcile the world to Jesus. Reconciliation is found in the wake of Jesus followers.

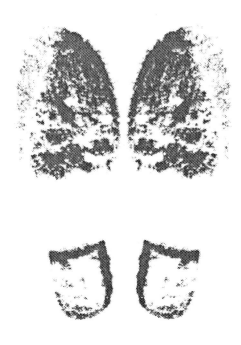

19 - Truth

After Jesus' capture and subsequent interrogation by the Chief Priest Caiaphas, he was taken to the Governor's palace where he was brought before Pilate.

"Pilate asked him, "So you are a king?" Jesus answered, "You say that I am a king. For this I was born, and for this I came into the world, to testify to the truth. Everyone who belongs to the truth listens to my voice." Pilate asked him, "What is truth?""[75]

Pilate's question is a question all of us must ask in life: what is truth?

In the Gospel of John, Jesus makes one of the boldest, if not the boldest statement ever made concerning truth.

"I am the way, and the truth, and the life. No one comes to the Father except through me."[76]

With this claim, Jesus draws a line in the sand so deep it has caused many to stumble and fall, unable to go further in their efforts to understand the truth that is Jesus. Truth is not some intellectual concept or topic for debate. The truth has a name and its name is Jesus.

Until the 16th century, the reality and truth of Jesus remained relatively unchallenged. However, modernity brought with it an onslaught of thinkers who attempted to dismantle and deconstruct not only the idea that Jesus was the truth, but that an ultimate truth even existed.

---

[75] John 18:37-38
[76] John 14:6

People such as Hobbes, Rousseau, Kant, Schopenhauer, Marx, Darwin, and Nietzsche, all questioned the truth that had inspired humanity for thousands of years. Their thinking was fueled by enlightenment revelations as they believed only verifiable and repeatable scientific results had the intellectual weight necessary to approach the realm of truth. Unfortunately, this scientific approach carries with it certain negative consequences. Scientific truth only retains authority until a new and better truth emerges. As a result, doubt and uncertainty hang like dark clouds over all these transient truths leaving moderns to look longingly toward the future when a new and better truth would be revealed.

Post-modernity continued to build upon the angst that entered the public square in modernity. As post-moderns, we find it hard to accept that there is only one truth. To even suggest this seems myopic and archaic. As a result, we find ourselves adrift on a stormy sea of self-doubt and false assurance in a climate that relativizes everything. What is true for you may not be true for someone else. In post-modernity, truth is relative and we must discover and construct truth within our own context while allowing space for someone else's truth to coexist.

However, truth is not some ephemeral theory or concept that rises to prominence one day and falls from favor the next. That is theory, not a truth. Truth has a name, its name is Jesus and his truth is not for the faint at heart.

As each of us struggles with our search for truth, know that God is not surprised or threatened by our questions, doubts, or attempts to create alternatives to the truth. We can remain certain that in spite of our wonderings and our wanderings, truth is comfortable in his skin.

20 - Struggle

"Very truly, I tell you, no one can enter the kingdom of God without being born of water and Spirit. What is born of the flesh is flesh, and what is born of the Spirit is spirit."[77]

Anyone who has ever given birth to a child, participated in the birth of a child, witnessed the birth of a child, or even heard stories of the birth of a child knows we do not come into this world easily. Being born of water is difficult. It is messy. It is a struggle.

For most of us, when we think of being born of the spirit, a much more peaceful experience comes to mind, something that happens in an instant, something unexplainable, something otherworldly.

But, what if Jesus' use of a birth metaphor to communicate the experience of being born again meant these two experiences have more in common than we first thought?

The Bible is replete with stories of those who wrestled with their faith... those whose lives were filled with all the earthy drama they could endure as they ran away from...or ran toward God.

Our personal stories of life are likely reflective of this reality. We have moments of great spiritual insight and confidence while at other times feel completely alone, abandoned in valleys of doubt and despair on this journey from who we were, to who we are to become.

---

[77] John 3:5-7

And so, the struggle is not something to be resisted or apologized for, but embraced with anxious anticipation as we participate in the birthing of a new spirit within us. Struggle is a sign Jesus followers are on the right path.

21 - Resurrection

"And we saw it, saw it all, everything he did in the land of the Jews and in Jerusalem where they killed him, hung him from a cross. But in three days God had him up, alive, and out where he could be seen."[78]

The truth of Christianity hinges on that final sentence.

The word for this is resurrection.

Most of us have been to the zoo. We have seen the miraculous variety of God's creation on display and have probably stood a few feet, maybe even inches away from some of nature's most dangerous animals...kept at a safe distance by thick glass, a cage, or perhaps a ditch, or a moat. These containers or barriers can give us the false impression that these animals are docile, safe, or perhaps domesticated, when in reality, if we were to meet them on their terms, in their natural habitat, with no barrier between us, the story would be different... the danger would be real...our place in this world clear.

The religious establishment of Jesus' day had a problem; Jesus could not be kept at a safe distance. His presence was a threat to their authority, their identity, and their way of life. They tried to tame and contain him with threats and accusations, but Jesus refused to be domesticated. They were not safe as long as Jesus was around. They concluded: an alive Jesus was a dangerous Jesus.

A dead Jesus, on the other hand, would be a safe Jesus.

---

[78] Acts: 10:36-40 (The Message)

A dead Jesus would be a Jesus who could be controlled, kept at a safe distance, held hostage in an earthly tomb; a place from which he could not threaten their authority, their identity, or their way of life.

A dead Jesus would be remembered as a good teacher, a prophet...maybe even a healer of the sick, or a defender of the poor; someone who would be studied, debated, and compared to others who had claimed to speak for God. A dead Jesus would be many things but one thing a dead Jesus could not be, was who people said he was...the Messiah.

What they had not planned on was a resurrected Jesus...the furthest thing from a safe Jesus.

A resurrected Jesus could not be kept at a safe distance.

A resurrected Jesus became the ultimate challenge to their authority, identity, and way of life.

A resurrected Jesus became more than a good teacher or prophet: more than a healer of the sick or an encourager of the downtrodden.

A resurrected Jesus became who he claimed he was: God in the flesh...the Messiah.

Knowing this, as followers of Jesus, we must look at the signs on the Jesus trail we are following to see what they tell us.

If the signs on our path reveal a Jesus who tends to agree with our perceptions, assumptions, and assessments, serving as evidence to back up our position; if our encounters or sightings of Jesus occur primarily in times of study or in moments of need; or if the Jesus we are tracking rarely asks us to do something outside of our comfort zone, then we are following a safe Jesus, a Jesus we have domesticated, a Jesus we can keep at a safe distance.

However, if we are on the trail of the resurrected Jesus, the signs will reveal we are following a Jesus that is alive and unpredictable, moving about in his natural habitat, refusing to be kept at a safe distance. This Jesus will challenge our identity, our authority, and our position in this world as he leads us to places where we must engage humanity on his terms and in his ways, getting our hands dirty in service of those Jesus loves.

The signs will reveal which Jesus we are following...

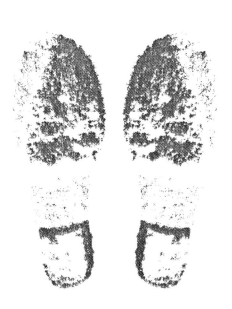

22 - Dance

Most of us, at some point, attended a high school dance. These annual rites of passage provide the stage on which young adult angst and false confidence often collide. Preparing for and getting to the event can be challenging enough, but once at the dance, the challenge of the primary question rises to prominence: "Would you like to dance?"

Being asked to dance affirms us and enlarges our soul. Not being asked to dance does the exact opposite. Not being asked to dance brings with it a series of unwelcome questions. Why didn't anyone ask me to dance? Is there something wrong with me? Am I invisible?

Being asked to dance, however, does not exempt us from questions... it just exposes us to different ones. Do I want to dance with this person? What are the implications of dancing with this person? Will everyone think we are an "item" if I dance with this person? Can I dance with this person? Will I have to slow dance with this person? Can I trust this person as a dancing partner? Will they stay on their side of my boundaries? Why are they asking me to dance? Do they like me or is this just a dance? If I dance with them, will my friends make fun of me? Or, are they asking me to dance on a dare?

There are a lot of questions contained within that single five-word question: "Would you like to dance?"

Jesus makes the following statement in Revelation 3:20.

"Listen! I am standing at the door, knocking; if you hear my voice and open the door, I will come in to you and eat with you, and you with me."

Jesus knocking at the door is an invitation, a question, an invitation to dance... and likewise, it brings a series of questions to the forefront. Do I want to dance with him? Can I trust him? Will he take over my life? Why would Jesus ask me to dance? Surely he must know who I am and my past? If I dance with him will I miss out on other things I might want to do? If I dance with him will my friends no longer be my friends?

There are a lot of questions contained within a knock at the door.

Jesus knocks on the door knowing full well the details of who lives at that address. He asks us to dance knowing there is indeed something wrong with us, something that only the dance can correct. Jesus asks us to dance knowing this dance could be difficult. He asks us to dance knowing who we have danced with in the past and all that entails. Jesus asks us to dance knowing we barely have strength to stand on our own. He asks us to dance knowing there is nothing we need more that to join him in the dance.

Perhaps we could rewrite Revelation 3:20 in the following manner... *Jesus stands at the door and asks...do you want to dance?*

Christians on the trail of Jesus are those who are learning to dance.

23 - Cross

The cross of Christ is one of our most recognizable Christian images; a sign above all signs. We see it on necklaces, earrings, tattoos, t-shirts, and stitched into jeans among other places. It is difficult to know whether the individuals adorning themselves with these crosses are doing so in an effort to express their Christian conviction or merely accessorizing their wardrobe. Either way, it's hard to be in a public space and not see a cross or two.

However, during the period when ancient Israel was under Roman rule, the cross was not a fashion accessory and its meaning was not up for debate; it was a sign of death. The cross was a device the culture used to enforce its will upon those who chose to behave in ways contrary to this will. It was an instrument of judgment, humiliation, and punishment as the objects of cultural condemnation were stripped of their dignity and allowed to die a slow, agonizing, and very public death.

It was on just such a cross the religious establishment attempted to extract its penalty on Jesus for claiming God as his father. The Pharisees, no doubt, hoped crucifying Jesus would strip him of his dignity, humiliate him, and convince his followers he was just an ordinary man who died an ordinary death. However, Jesus was no ordinary man.

When his crucifixion was complete, Jesus was placed in a tomb and its entrance was sealed. Due to claims the tomb would not be able to hold Jesus and he would rise from the grave alive, guards were posted at its entrance to prevent his disciples from helping this ordinary man somehow seem extraordinary. However, something extraordinary happened; the tomb was unable to contain Jesus; he was who he said he was; Jesus rose to life and out of the grave.

Prior to Jesus' capture and crucifixion, he made a statement to his disciples that, at the time, was likely confusing:

"If any want to become my followers, let them deny themselves and take up their cross and follow me."[79]

While the cross Jesus carried was made of wood, ours is not. Instead, ours is a cross constructed of shame, humiliation, and failure…a cross crafted from failed expectations and hurtful intentions. We are called to take up this cross and follow Jesus on a journey that leads us to the foot of his cross; a place we come face to face with our Savior. It is here we lay down our crosses.

After Jesus' crucifixion, the cross took on new meaning. What was once a symbol of judgment became a symbol of forgiveness. What was once a symbol of humiliation became a symbol of grace. What was once a symbol of death became a symbol of new life.

At the cross we do experience a death, but it is a death to the things of death so we can live for the things of life.

All paths toward Jesus involve two crosses: his and ours.

These paths cross at the cross.

---

[79] Mark 8:34

24 - At-One-Ment

In this Book of Signs, a crowdsourcing participant chose to express the word we would typically recognize as atonement in the less familiar form of at-one-ment which necessitates we shine a slightly different light on this sign post.

For those of us who like to be out in the midst of God's creation, working in our gardens or perhaps hiking and camping, there can be those special times when this experience becomes so pure, so humbling, and so captivating, that we feel part of God's creation, connected to it, not distanced from it, not superior to it or beneath it, but fully alive and intertwined within it. When this happens, we might say we feel "at one" with creation. We might also express this as an experience of at-one-ment.

Atonement, as most of us know, refers to the process whereby we are made right with God: covered or protected from judgment. The book of Leviticus is filled with many examples of atonement ceremonies in which the members of the tribe of Israel brought sacrifices to the priests who make atonement on their behalf.

"Thus the priest shall make atonement on your behalf, and you shall be forgiven."[80]

These acts of atonement were repeated at various times throughout the year since sin was ongoing and one needed to atone for ones sins on a regular basis.

---

[80] Leviticus 4:31

69

The concept of a central, one-time-only, atoning event is essential to Christian theology: *"All have sinned and fall short of the glory of God; they are now justified by his grace as a gift, through the redemption that is in Christ Jesus, whom God put forward as a sacrifice of atonement by his blood, effective through faith."*[81]

With Jesus' atoning sacrifice, through faith, we are brought back into good standing, once and for all...back into proper relationship with God. Our sins are covered. We are protected from judgment. We are no longer separated from God by the chasm of sin.

The experience of atonement, of this removal of separation between ourselves and God can be seen as a kind of at-one-ment, similar to the experience of being at-one with creation in that our experience of God becomes so pure, so humbling, and so captivating, that we truly feel a part of and connected to God.

Experiencing this at-one-ment confirms the path we are following is leading toward the one through which all things came into being[82] and in whom we find our home: Jesus.

---

[81] Romans 3:23-25
[82] John 1:3

25 - Possible

Christianity redefines the landscape of possible.

- The virgin birth of a child who is both fully human and fully God... possible?

- Someone rising from the dead...possible?

- Forgiveness beyond imagination...possible?

- An eternal life beyond what we see and experience here on earth...possible?

- God knew us before we were born and has a plan for our lives...possible?

You get the idea...

Christianity ignites our imaginations, inspires our dreams, and informs our theology with a new understanding of what is possible.

*"Children, how hard it is to enter the kingdom of God! It is easier for a camel to go through the eye of a needle than for someone who is rich to enter the kingdom of God." They were greatly astounded and said to one another, "Then who can be saved?" Jesus looked at them and said, "For mortals it is impossible, but not for God; for God all things are **possible**."*[83]

Jesus was the living, breathing, possibility of God. He lived past the edge of what most of us would consider possible. And, in his darkest hour...the moment of his greatest doubt, Jesus asked God to consider a possibility.

---

[83] Mark 10:24-27 (emphasis added)

*"He took with him Peter and James and John, and began to be distressed and agitated. And he said to them, "I am deeply grieved, even to death; remain here, and keep awake." And going a little farther, he threw himself on the ground and prayed that, if it were **possible**, the hour might pass from him. He said, "Abba, Father, for you all things are **possible**; remove this cup from me; yet, not what I want, but what you want.""*[84]

In this prayer, Jesus expressed a desperate desire for another possibility, another way to bridge this chasm between God and his creation. But, as Jesus prayed his request, he acknowledged the possibility that his best option was to submit to God, the Father in whom all things are possible.

As followers of Jesus, when we find ourselves in the midst of a situation we wish we could avoid or carrying a burden that seems too heavy to bear, we must remember, the best solution is a Jesus solution: submit it to the God of the possible, for *"All things are possible with God."*[85]

---

[84] Mark 14:33-36 (emphasis added)
[85] Mark 10:27 (NIV)

26 - Messiah

It is tempting to combine our crowdsourced words of Messiah and Christ into one entry on this list of trail markers. However, to do so would not only subvert the will of our crowd, but would also require us to overlook or ignore a subtle distinction.

The word Messiah comes from the Hebrew word מָשִׁיחַ or mashiach, which means anointed. The New Testament, however, was not written in Hebrew. It was written in Greek, primarily for a non-Hebrew speaking audience. Therefore, the Greek word Χριστός or *christos* was used in the New Testament to indicate *anointed*. It is from this language we get the title Jesus Christ or Jesus the Christ... Jesus The Anointed One.[86]

Interestingly, the various translations of the New Testament are not consistent in their translation of the word *christos*. In some instances, the word *christos* is translated as the word Messiah while in others it is translated as Christ. For example, the book of Matthew begins with the phrase *"An account of the genealogy of Jesus the Messiah, the son of David, the son of Abraham."*[87] While the Greek text used the word *christos* in this passage, here it is translated as Messiah. Translating *christos* as Messiah in this instance makes contextual sense in that Matthew is connecting Jesus to the Hebrew expectation of a deliverer... a mashiach. However, as Christianity expanded and reached out to a non-Jewish audience, the term *christos* or Christ rose in prominence.

---

[86] If you are reading this book you probably knew this, but just in case... :)
[87] Matthew 1:1

Why this preoccupation with the distinction between the words Messiah and Christ? Here is why. The authors of our canon were very deliberate in the way they used words. Words had meaning and the right meaning was important. When we do not pause for a moment on a word in an attempt to understand the depth of meaning contained within that word, we reduce it, we take it for granted, we limit our understanding, and we increase the likelihood of our misunderstanding.

The word Messiah is an ancient word that carries with it the expectation of a future deliverer. The word Christ builds upon that history to announce the arrival of that deliverer to the world in language they can understand. Together they identify the hope of all creation, illuminating a path that stretches backward and forward into eternity…a path all followers of Jesus must travel.

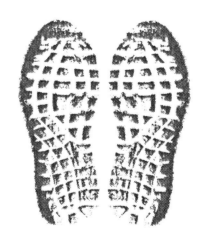

27 - Fruit

The Bible is a book filled with fruit. Fruit nourishes and fruit betrays. Fruits of the womb are dedicated while first fruits are offered. Fruit can reveal God's faithfulness and provision while, at the same time, a lack of fruit can be a sign of God's displeasure. Fruit and the kingdom are connected at their core.

The New Testament tells of a curious encounter between Jesus and a fruitless tree... a fig tree to be precise. While on the way to Jerusalem with the disciples, Jesus approaches a fig tree expecting to find something for breakfast. However, when he finds no figs, in a moment of what seems like uncharacteristic behavior, Jesus curses the fig tree, telling it *"no one is going to eat fruit from you again-ever."*[88] On their return trip from Jerusalem, Peter points out the fig tree Jesus cursed has shriveled up and died. Apparently, there are consequences to a fruit-less existence.

"I am the true vine, and my Father is the vine grower. He removes every branch in me that bears no fruit. Every branch that bears fruit he prunes to make it bear more fruit."[89]

The purpose of the fig tree was to bear fruit. It was not bearing fruit, and as such, was not fulfilling its purpose. Therefore...it was removal time.

But, lets go a little further. Fruit is the part of the plant that contains the seeds. Fruit can be delicious, but the generation of delicious fruit is not the end game. Seeds are the end game. More fruit is the end game. Future generations are the end game.

---

[88] Mark 11:14 (The Message)
[89] John 15:1-2

In the case of the fig tree, each fig can contain between 30 to 1600 seeds. Each of these seeds has the potential to become a fig tree that in turn, if it is *fruit-full,* can result in the production of thousands and thousands of figs. Perhaps Jesus' anger at the fruit-less fig tree was not the result of low blood sugar, but instead revealed his frustration with the future harvest that would never be.

While there are certain benefits associated with a life of faith, becoming a Christian is not the end game. It is not the destination at which we can kick back and enjoy the fruits of our labors. Instead, its the point at which we are grafted onto the vine... the point at which we begin to generate fruit... fruit that is not only pleasing to God but fruit that plants seeds of faith in others...fruit that points them toward God so they can bear fruit of their own.

Followers on the path of Jesus are called to be *fruit-full,* seeding the world with fruits of the spirit. As such we can expect a little pruning, which can be painful, but pruning is better than the alternatives.

28 - Hospitality/Hospitable

Some people have the gift of hospitality. They are good at creating safe environments in which people can feel welcome, be themselves, and enjoy one another. Typically, these individuals have a circle of friends who like accepting their invitations.

Paul talks about the need for Christians to extend hospitality, but a slightly different kind of hospitality...a hospitality that extends beyond those close to us...a hospitality to strangers.[90]

Hospitality extended to a group of friends is one thing, but hospitality offered to strangers can be a little more difficult, even for the hospitable ones. Extending hospitality to strangers places us in the position of creating environments in which those we don't like, don't know, or maybe even disagree with are welcomed and accepted in hopes that we discover one another's humanity and depart as friends.

Nouwen suggests the intent of hospitality "is not to change people, but to offer them space where change can take place. It is not to bring men and women over to our side, but to offer freedom not disturbed by dividing lines."[91]

In their book Unchristian, David Kinnaman and Gabe Lyons suggest those outside the Church see those within the Church as something less that hospitable. One of those they interviewed put it this way: "Most people I meet assume that Christian means very conservative, entrenched in their thinking,

---

[90] Romans 12:13
[91] Henri J M. Nouwen, *Reaching Out: The Three Movements of the Spiritual Life* (Garden City, N.Y.: Image Books, 1986), 55.

antigay, anti-choice, angry, violent, illogical, empire builders; they want to convert everyone, and they generally cannot live peacefully with anyone who doesn't believe what they believe."[92] We may not want to own this, or we may even tend to disagree, but we cannot deny, in this light, as a people, Christians do not sound very hospitable.

If Christians are to become the hospitable ones, in our lives and in our churches, we are going to need to erase the lines between you and me, between us and them, between ourselves and the other and create spaces where "strangers can cast off their strangeness and become our fellow human beings."[93]

While on the trail as followers of Jesus, we may find ourselves in hostile or in-hospitable environments. But, as Christians, let us never be guilty of anything less that being hospitable to those we meet on the trail.

---

[92] David Kinnaman and Gabe Lyons, *Unchristian: What a New Generation Really Thinks About Christianity-- and Why It Matters* (Grand Rapids, Mich.: Baker Books, 2007), 26.
[93] Nouwen, *Reaching Out*, 65.

29 - Meal

Most of us are at least somewhat familiar with the prayer Jesus taught the disciples we know as the Lord's Prayer.

Our Father which art in heaven, Hallowed be thy name.

Thy kingdom come. Thy will be done in earth, as it is in heaven.

Give us this day our daily bread.

And forgive us our debts, as we forgive our debtors.

And lead us not into temptation, but deliver us from evil:

For thine is the kingdom, and the power, and the glory, forever. Amen.[94]

For the sake of our discussion, we need to pause for a moment and consider one of the stanzas in this prayer…the only one that is uniquely identified as a daily need…the request for daily bread.

The prayer does not request the kingdom to come daily or God's will to be done daily on the earth as it is in heaven, nor does it ask for our debts to be forgiven daily or that we be delivered from temptation daily. Bread is unique in its identification as…daily.

One could easily argue that if we were to pray this prayer every day, all of our requests would indeed be daily. While logical and accurate, this does not shine any light on why bread was the only request in the prayer with a "daily" directly attached.

---

[94] Matthew 6:9-13 (King James)

Culturally, we might be tempted to view this as perhaps speaking to the poor living conditions of those who were/are (in modern terminology) "food insecure" in that they might only have access to provision in daily portions, unable to stock or store away the ingredients necessary to provide bread for more than a day. This would make sense to a certain degree, however, it does not ring true with the bulk of Jesus' messages in that he tended to speak to the human condition rather than to a particular socio-economic class or group. So then; why "daily" bread?

To better understand this, lets first look at the story of the Israelites journey away from Egypt. While their freedom was new and their memories of captivity fresh, they got hungry and began to complain. Growling stomachs apparently caused them to long wistfully for their days back in Egypt where at least their stomachs were full, even though their lives were full of misery.

In response to their complaints, the Lord spoke to Moses: *"I am going to rain bread from heaven for you, and each day the people shall go out and gather enough for that day."*[95] Here we find a promise of daily bread, bread that would nourish them for only a single day since this bread would go bad if they tried to stockpile these resources.[96] This daily bread reinforced Israel's complete dependence on God while sustaining them on their journey for many years.

Now fast forward to the New Testament where Jesus tells his disciples: *"I am the living bread that came down from heaven. Whoever eats of this bread will live forever."*[97] Here Jesus makes the connection between the bread from

---

[95] Exodus 16:4
[96] On that Sabbath they could gather two days provision.
[97] John 6:51

heaven God provided the nation of Israel with this new revelation of Jesus as the living bread, the bread from heaven that makes possible everlasting life.

And so, when we pray this prayer asking for our daily bread, we are doing more than asking for food for the day, we are also aligning ourselves with the source of life and acknowledging our complete and utter dependence on Jesus, the bread of the New Covenant that came down from heaven so that we might live.

The scent of this meal must never leave our nostrils if we, as followers of Jesus are to stay true to the path.

30 - Inhabit

To inhabit means to "live in or occupy a place or an environment."[98] When we inhabit a space, we are influenced by the place we inhabit and in turn exert some degree of influence on that space as well. Influence is a two way street.

For example, someone who lives nestled away in a lush mountain paradise will have a considerably different life experience than someone who might live in the barren surroundings of the Sahara desert. The physical location, culture, and individuals of those environments are quite distinct, enabling vastly different life experiences and opportunities. However, in these or any environment we find ourselves, we are also capable of influencing the spaces we inhabit as our presence impacts not only that particular locale, but its individuals and culture as well.

As Christians, we participate in this give and take of our habitations with one very unique distinction. We not only inhabit, but we are inhabited. An invited guest has taken up residence within us and inhabits that residence.

"The mystery in a nutshell is just this: Christ is in you."[99]

In other words: Christ inhabits you.

As the one who inhabits us, Jesus influences us. Everything we do, think, feel, and say comes under the influence of the one who inhabits us. We could say; Christians are under the influence...the influence of Christ who lives

---

[98]

http://oxforddictionaries.com/definition/american_english/inhabit?region=us&q=inhabit

[99] Colossians 1:27 (The Message)

within us. In turn, when followers of Jesus inhabit a place or a culture, we exert a Jesus influence upon that culture, as everything around us comes under the influence of the one who inhabits our being...under the influence of Jesus.

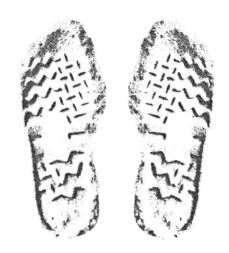

31 - Humility

The Bible is pretty clear as to the role humility should play in the life of Jesus followers.

"As God's chosen ones, holy and beloved, clothe yourselves with compassion, kindness, humility, meekness, and patience."[100]

"Do nothing from selfish ambition or conceit, but in humility regard others as better than yourselves."[101]

Humility is a hard sell in a culture where individual accomplishment is celebrated and success is achieved by climbing one's way to the top, oftentimes stepping over others rather that stepping aside to clear the path for their ascent. In fact, humility in life and the marketplace can be seen as a weakness, a vulnerability that makes the humble ones easy targets, weaker members of the pack easily taken out.

A life of humility comes with certain challenges. However, the cultural difficulties for Christians associated with living a humble life seem to pale when compared with the following: *"All of you must clothe yourselves with humility in your dealings with one another, for 'God opposes the proud, but gives grace to the humble.'"*[102]

While it would be difficult for us to define exactly how this opposition might manifest, most of us would agree, if given the choice, we would prefer to be the recipients of God's grace rather than find ourselves facing God's opposition.

---

[100] Colossians 3:12
[101] Philippians 2:3
[102] 1 Peter 5:5

Christianity is enabled through God's grace. We do not earn our way into a kingdom life. We are incapable of doing so. If our works could gain us entry, we would have reason to boast or look down upon others who could not master the requirements for admission. But, our reconciliation with God does not result from our actions. It results from the actions of another...the actions of Jesus. We are no more capable of being good enough for God than any other human. Therefore, as we do our best to follow in the footsteps of Jesus, we should conduct ourselves with appropriate humility, for it is the humble that will find grace to carry on.

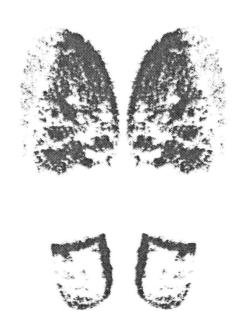

32 - Repentant

When we hear the word "repent," one of the first stories that likely comes to mind is that of John the Baptist. As we know, John arrived on the scene early in the Gospels, described as a man living in the wilderness, clothed in camel hair, and dining on locust while announcing his message for all to hear: *"Repent, for the kingdom of heaven has come near."*[103] The kingdom was indeed near as many took his message to heart and were baptized by John in the river.

The kingdom of heaven was near another day when the scribes and Pharisees brought a woman before Jesus who had been caught in the act of adultery. They reminded Jesus the law of Moses demanded they stone such women. They asked Jesus his opinion as a test, hoping his answer might reveal an inconsistency in Jesus' teaching as a way to discredit him. Jesus responded in a very Jesus like manner: *"Let anyone among you who is without sin be the first to throw a stone at her."*[104] It's not hard to imagine the disappointment of the Pharisees that day when the ground on which their theology stood shifted in a instant as there were probably more than a few in that crowd who would like to have participated in a good stoning as a way to somehow validate themselves as those above such accusations.

However, much to their disappointment, one by one, the members of the crowd walked away, leaving Jesus alone with the woman. He asked her: *""Woman, where are they? Has no one condemned you?" She said, "No one, sir." And Jesus said, "Neither do I condemn you. Go your way, and from now*

---

[103] Matthew 3:2
[104] John 8:7

on do not sin again.""[105] In other words, repent, turn away from your sin and change your ways.

Sometimes repentance gets a bad rap when we define it as only a call to stop doing something...when it is only about our turning away from that which has become too familiar. But, we must remember, one cannot turn away from something without turning toward something else. When we repent, we redirect, we change course. Repent is more than a *stop* sign, it is also a *go* sign, but a *go* sign in a different direction.

To repent, the woman in the story had to turn away from the shame of her actions and the voices of condemnation emanating from her accusers, turning her attention instead toward Jesus, the one who spoke healing and forgiveness into her life and future.

Repentance requires a change of course... a revising of our trajectory, away from a path that leads us to destruction and in a new direction that leads us toward life. Followers of Jesus should be the repentant ones, always aligning and redirecting our thoughts, our hearts, and our actions toward Jesus; the true north of our faith.

---

[105] John 8:10-11

33 - Community/Connected

When Jesus began his public ministry, he selected 12 individuals to connect with in community. They lived together, ate together, traveled together, and learned together. Their example is our primary model of how discipleship is worked out in community and connection with other followers of Jesus.

Western culture does not lean easily into this type of community, as its primary inclination tends to be more individualistic in nature. Geert Hofstede has conducted extensive research on cultures around to world and as a result has developed a metric we can use to compare these cultures based upon 5 measurements: power distance, individualism, masculinity, uncertainty avoidance, and long-term orientation.[106] For our purposes we will look at the measurement of individualism.

Through Hofstede's research, he was able to assign a numerical value reflecting the degree to which a culture embraces individuality; the higher the number, the more individualistic the culture. A high score on the individualistic (IDV) scale would suggest a culture in which loose ties between individuals are predominant and where everyone is expected to primarily care for themselves and secondarily their immediate family.[107] A low score on the IDV scale would indicate a more collectivist culture in which individuals would be active participants in a larger family unit which included not just immediate family but also aunt/uncles etc.[108]

---

[106] http://www.geerthofstede.nl/culture/dimensions-of-national-cultures.aspx
[107] Ibid.
[108] Ibid.

Individualistic or collectivistic tendencies tend to determine the way individuals engage or distance themselves from inter-dependent relationships. The more individualistic the individual, the more inclined they would be to forge their own path as compared to working for the good of a group. The following list shows how various nations scored on the Hofstede IDV scale.[109]

United States - 91

Australia - 90

Great Britain - 89

Sweden - 71

Germany - 67

Israel - 54

Mexico - 30

China – 20

As we might expect, Western countries typically score higher on individualism. Therefore, efforts to connect with one another as an enactment of Biblical community are going to be problematic for Western cultures while less challenging for countries ranking lower on the IDV scale such as China or Mexico. In spite of its ease or difficulty however, the Bible calls us to a connected life… a life in which we live in community with one another.

---

[109] http://www.geerthofstede.nl/research--vsm.aspx The top number of the scale is 100.

The Apostle Paul paints a beautiful picture in 1 Corinthians 12 of the role community plays in the life of a Christian with his Body of Christ metaphor. In Paul's illustration, he compares the body of believers to the literal Body of Christ. He tells of the interconnectedness of the various parts and how they are dependent upon one another for survival. He also tells us of the folly associated with believing an individual can exist disconnected from the support of the rest of body.

In spite of the ways in which Western culture invites and encourages us to go it alone, to make our own way, to forge our own path, followers of Jesus are dependent on one another for survival. To discern if the path you are following is the path of Jesus, lift your eyes from the trail and look around. Are you walking alone or walking with a community?

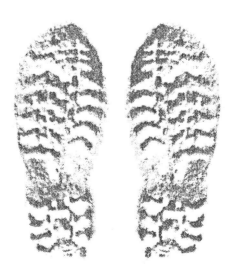

34 - Apathetic

Finding a word like apathetic on our list of trail markers is kind of like seeing a recent family photo hanging on the wall and noticing a piece of food in our teeth. The picture does not confirm the image of ourselves we would like to present to the world. But, there it is, in all its glory, revealing that we are…in fact…not perfect.[110]

Apathy is defined as lack of feeling or emotion, lack of interest or concern.[111] Are we willing to acknowledge and accept apathetic as an indicator that we are following Jesus?

In pursuit of an answer, we must ask another question: are we really being apathetic if our actions reflect the true nature of our beliefs?

It has been argued that when our practices seem to fall short of our beliefs, rather than revealing a certain apathy toward those beliefs, this instead, reveals the true nature of our beliefs.[112] (Oops…is that some food in our teeth?)

This proposal suggests that when we do not come to the aid of a neighbor in need, it is not because we are apathetic to their needs, but instead, it is because we do not actually believe we need to come to the aid of the neighbor. Or, when we do not come alongside the homeless or abused in our community in an attempt to remedy their situation, it is not because we are apathetic to their plight, it is because we do not really believe Jesus' instructions that we should.

---

[110] Isn't crowdsourcing fun!
[111] http://www.merriam-webster.com/dictionary/apathy
[112] Peter Rollins, *Insurrection* (Nashville, Tenn.: Howard Books, 2011), 92.

In this view, as Christians, we are not being apathetic to the needs around us, we just don't believe what we say we do.

If this is the case, Christian apathy is not a trail marker to be followed, rather it is a condition that reveals the need for a re-alignment of our behaviors with one of the bedrock tenants of our faith:

"You shall love the Lord your God with all your heart, and with all your soul, and with all your strength, and with all your mind; and your neighbor as yourself."[113]

As Christians, we are called to love God and love our neighbors in the same manner in which we care for ourselves. We feed ourselves when we are hungry. We clothe ourselves when we need clothing. We work to provide housing for ourselves when we are in need of housing. These are not difficult decisions when considering ourselves, so they should not be difficult decisions when concerning our neighbors.

If we were to adhere to what Jesus said were the two greatest commandments of our faith, the "apathetic" trail marker would no longer be an indicator of the presence of Jesus followers. This is a goal, about which, we should not find ourselves apathetic.

---

[113] Matthew 22:36-40, Mark 12:29:30, Luke 10:27

35 - Justice

Oftentimes, when we think about justice, we think of it in terms of punishment for a crime or of making restitution for a wrong. This is easy to do because the Old Testament was pretty clear on how justice was supposed to work.

"Anyone who kills a human being shall be put to death. Anyone who kills an animal shall make restitution for it, life for life. Anyone who maims another shall suffer the same injury in return: fracture for fracture, eye for eye, tooth for tooth; the injury inflicted is the injury to be suffered."[114]

However, Jesus radically redefined our understanding of justice:

"You have heard that it was said, 'An eye for an eye and a tooth for a tooth.' But I say to you, Do not resist an evildoer. But if anyone strikes you on the right cheek, turn the other also; and if anyone wants to sue you and take your coat, give your cloak as well; and if anyone forces you to go one mile, go also the second mile."[115]

These two approaches stand in stark contrast to one another, and yet oftentimes we cling to the desire to dole out Old Testament justice to others while, at the same time, claiming New Testament justice for ourselves. This may be human nature to some degree, but as Christians, we have a new nature and this new nature should reflect Jesus justice on those around us?

Therefore, when we as followers on the trail of Jesus encourage, counsel, feed, clothe, rescue, or help provide paths out of homelessness, prostitution, or

---

[114] Leviticus 24:17-20
[115] Matthew 5:38-41

slavery, we become the practitioners of true justice, justice that sacrifices rather than retaliates, justice which gives rather than takes, and justice which is shared rather than demanded.

Justice through one (Jesus)... justice for all.

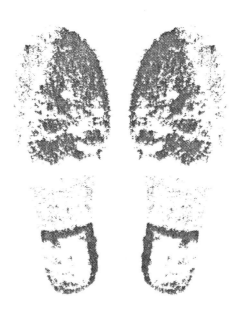

36 - Great Romance

AMC maintains a crowdsourcing site where people can vote on the greatest romance movies of all time.[116] Currently the distant leader is Gone With the Wind, followed by Casablanca, Sense and Sensibility, Now Voyager, and the Notebook. Further down the list you will find Sleepless in Seattle, Love Actually, You Got Mail, and of course Titanic. Most of us are familiar with these movies. Having not seen all of these movies, I cannot say the tried and true romance story of *boy meets girl, boy loses girl, boy gets girl back again* is the theme of each of the movies, but I am guessing it is in there in some way, shape, or form since this is the standard formula for making a great romance movie.

The Bible tells the story of another great romance in which we have a repeating theme: God gets humanity, God loses humanity, God gets humanity, God loses humanity. Etc. Etc. Etc. Now granted, ultimately God does not lose humanity, but there is an ongoing theme of separation and reunification that occurs again and again. However, there is a slight twist to this story.

In the great romance story of the Bible, God gets humanity, God is separated from humanity, and then God builds a bridge across which humanity is free to travel as a way to restore the relationship forever. Jesus is that bridge.

And so, as followers of Jesus, we must ask ourselves; are we creating obstacles or barriers to the great romance or clearing paths and building bridges? Paths and bridges are signs the one we are following is Jesus.

---

[116] http://www.amc.com/movie-guide/50-greatest-romantic-movies

37 - Servants/Server

A quick scan of the top 100 jobs in the United States reveals a variety of diverse and apparently desired professions. We see everything on this list from Orthodontist to Survey Researcher...from Computer Analyst to Nail Technician, but nowhere on the list do we find the occupation of servant.[117] I guess that makes sense, not many little kids when asked what they want to be when they grow up say "servant" and if they did a little parental career steering would likely come into play. However, as unpopular as a career being a servant might be, this is exactly the calling Jesus set before us...that is if we want to be great in the kingdom over-and-above great in the world.

"Whoever wishes to become great among you must be your servant, and whoever wishes to be first among you must be slave of all. For the Son of Man came not to be served but to serve, and to give his life a ransom for many."[118]

Jesus provided an illustration of what it meant to be a servant to the disciples one evening by washing their feet. It is easy for us to overlook the awkwardness of this situation... God in the flesh, down on his knees, bathing the dirty feet of his friends. Peter was apparently uncomfortable, he protested, claiming he would never let Jesus humble himself in such a manner. But, Jesus nudged Peter into compliance by telling him that unless he washed his feet, Peter would have no part of Jesus. Peter did an about face, as Peter was known to do.

Jesus then asked the disciples if they knew what he had done, or in other words, do you know why I did this? Jesus explained: *"You call me Teacher and Lord—and you are right, for that is what I am. So if I, your Lord and*

---

[117] http://money.usnews.com/careers/best-jobs/rankings/the-100-best-jobs

Teacher, have washed your feet, you also ought to wash one another's feet. For I have set you an example, that you also should do as I have done to you. Very truly, I tell you, servants are not greater than their master, nor are messengers greater than the one who sent them. If you know these things, you are blessed if you do them."[119]

This lesson must have impacted the authors of the New Testament because in their writings, we see them introducing themselves not as powerful, or occupying positions of prominence, but instead, as servants.

I, Paul, became a servant of this gospel.[120]

James, a servant of God and of the Lord Jesus Christ.[121]

Simeon Peter, a servant and apostle of Jesus Christ.[122]

Jude, a servant of Jesus Christ and brother of James.[123]

The revelation of Jesus Christ, which God gave him to show his servants what must soon take place; he made it known by sending his angel to his servant John.[124]

Christians on the trail of Jesus are called to be servants, serving God by serving one another. It is in this servant life that the trail of Jesus is revealed.

---

[118] Mark 10:43-45
[119] John 13:13-17
[120] Colossians 1:23
[121] James 1:1
[122] 2 Peter 1:1
[123] Jude 1:1
[124] Revelation 1:1

38 - Inclusive

In recent years, the term *inclusive* has come to be associated with those who attempt to maintain what could be considered a politically correct stance on many of the highly emotional issues that tend to divide us. Being inclusive is sometimes seen as the response to the post-modern revelation that there is no ultimate right or wrong, only matters of personal choice to be lived and embraced. This predilection toward inclusiveness is seen as something new and resonates among the voices of those on the fringe when directed toward those in what could be considered the mainstream. However, the idea of inclusiveness is not a new idea. If anyone is the definition of inclusive, it is Jesus. And, if any worldview should be the definition of inclusive it would be the Christian worldview if we are to believe what we read in the New Testament. .

Inclusiveness is one of the things that put Jesus on the business side of the Pharisees. Mark 2 tells of Jesus' attending a dinner at Levi's house in which the guest list would have no doubt been seen as "inclusive." The Pharisees asked: *"Why does he eat with tax collectors and sinners?"*[125] In their day, tax collectors were considered dishonest and ritually unclean due to their association with Gentiles.[126] Jesus' mere association with these individuals challenged the religious conscience of the time serving to provoke animosity between Jesus and the disapproving religious establishment.[127] Jesus no doubt overheard their exclusionary grumbling and responded: *"Those who are well*

---

[125] Mark 2:16
[126] Harold W. Attridge, ed., *The HarperCollins Study Bible: Fully Revised and Updated,* Rev Upd ed. (San Francisco, Calif.: HarperOne, 2006), 905.
[127] Ibid.

have no need of a physician, but those who are sick; I have come to call not the righteous but sinners."[128]

Jesus seemed to enjoy challenging the socially accepted barriers of the day. Another one of these barriers had to do with the culture's approach to individuals with leprosy. Leprosy was a dreaded and deadly disease and until 1960 it was believed to be incurable.[129] The Hebrew Bible contains very strict rules concerning those who had or thought they might have leprosy. The unfortunate victims of this disease were considered unclean and forced to live on the margins of society. They were to dress in ways that identified them as lepers, and as such, no one was to touch or come near them. The culture was not inclusive of lepers, however Jesus was.

Mark tells the story. *"A leper came to him begging him, and kneeling he said to him, 'If you choose, you can make me clean.' Moved with pity, Jesus stretched out his hand and touched him, and said to him, 'I do choose. Be made clean! Immediately the leprosy left him, and he was made clean.'"*[130] With a healing touch another barrier was broken.

This begs the question: who are the lepers of today? Who are those that are banished from society or from social interaction? The first group in recent history that comes to mind are AIDS victims. As society became aware of this disease, the unfortunate victims of AIDS became the new untouchables. Now, as we have learned more about how this disease is transmitted, we are re-opening doors that were previously closed to its victims. However, many are still unwilling to invite them back into the mainstream of society as they

---

[128] Mark 2:17

[129] Geoffrey W. Bromiley, *The International Standard Bible Encyclopedia: Vol. 3* (Grand Rapids, MI: Eerdmans Pub Co, 1995), 103.

[130] Mark 1:40-42

remain seemingly content to let its victims suffer the consequences of their behaviors.

However, one does not have to be diseased to join the ranks of the untouchables. The lepers of today can also be the homeless, the addicted, the young and pregnant, the LBGT population, or even those who have breached our trust and now must assume a position among those to whom we direct our exclusionary impulses... as if excluding is a way to punish or somehow maintain our immunity to falling victim to the same circumstances.

Whenever we are tempted to distance ourselves from those we consider less than desirable, we need only remember the words of Paul from the book of Romans: *"For all have sinned, and come short of the glory of God."*[131] All have sinned and find themselves lacking. For some, these battle scars are visible and easily identifiable...for others their failings are found in the recesses of their hearts. The recognition and acceptance of this universal reality locates us in close proximity to one another as we are included in the ranks of many an untouchable follower of Jesus who found their salvation at the foot of the cross.

---

[131] Romans 3:23

39 - Human

As humans, we see the world from a human perspective. We do not know how to interpret our lives and our world in any other manner. This is at least partially revealed by the way in which we assign human characteristics, tendencies, or names to things that are not human, and in many cases not alive. We name our cars, computers, pets, and plants with names of either gender while those names assigned to boats or airplanes are typically feminine because... "She's a beauty." But, in spite of our efforts to humanize our world and those things we interact with, these objects remain somewhat less that human. So, what does it mean to be human?

Genesis 1:26 tells of God's intention for His human creation: *"Then God said, 'Let us make humankind in our image, according to our likeness.'"* However, in spite of God's high expectations for humans to reflect the divine, our humanness most often serves as a way to distinguish or illuminate the difference between ourselves and the perfection of God. After all, the phrase "I'm only human" is typically voiced as a way to excuse our somewhat less than divine behavior.

But, as humans, we are not sentenced to a life subject to the lesser attributes of our humanness. Instead, we are the recipients of a living reminder and example of God's aspirations for his human creation...Jesus. Jesus existed as both fully human and fully divine. In theology this is known as the hypostatic union. Attempts to arrive at an understanding of this reality have fueled many debates over the centuries. However, in spite of our inability to fully grasp this theological paradox, the hypostatic union between God and humanity expressed in Jesus provides us with the best example of God's vision for humanity. Therefore, when we walk and act in ways that reflect a life envisioned by Jesus, we are fully manifesting what it means to be human... we are expressing what it means to be created in the image or "likeness" of God. Being human is not an excuse to indulge our more base instincts, but rather it serves as an invitation for followers of Jesus to live out a human expression of our divine calling.

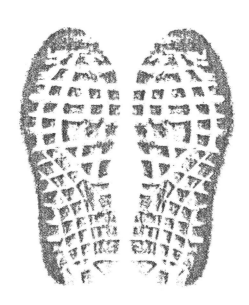

40 - Garden

A garden is a plot of land where various fruits and vegetables are planted and tended as they grow to produce their bounty. Gardens do not rise up of their own volition. A garden is intentional. Yes, fruits and vegetables may spring forth from the ground in unexpected places but when they do, we do not call that a garden, we just call that good fortune.

A garden necessitates a caretaker who cultivates the garden. It requires someone who has the garden's best interests at heart. If the caretaker puts forth the effort and takes good care of the garden, it will thrive and bring forth the bounty for which it was intended.

The book of Genesis tells a gardening story. In the story, God creates a garden known as Eden. After creating this garden God said, *"'Let the earth put forth vegetation: plants yielding seed, and fruit trees of every kind on earth that bear fruit with the seed in it.' And it was so."*[132] But gardens don't take care of themselves, they require a gardener...a caretaker. So, God created humanity and placed them on the earth with a purpose... to *"till it and keep it."*[133] From this we can ascertain humanity's original and primary purpose was to care for and cultivate the garden.

The meaning contained within this story may seem a little more relevant to an agricultural society than to those living in a predominantly industrialized culture. But, if our original intent was to be gardeners, how might this speak to us today?

---

[132] Gen 1:11
[133] Gen 2:15

First of all, we are the gardeners of our own lives. God has seeded us with a variety of gifts and abilities. These abilities come to fruition as we exercise them in pursuit of the dreams and aspirations God has planted within us. As we develop and nourish them, we are coming into alignment with God's general and specific purpose for our lives. But these tools are not for our own edification nor are they developed or fulfilled in isolation. Rather they only come to fruition in relationship with one another. A single plant is not a garden.

As we care for our own gardens, we are also called to nourish and care for the gardens of others. This care can manifest in providing basic needs such as food, clothing, or shelter for our fellow gardeners. Or, it can be expressed in the shared work of weeding, tilling and pruning one another's gardens. As we work alongside one another, the sharing of gardening stories encourages the success of each other's gardens. We can also help new gardeners as we provide them with the benefit or our gardening experience; helping them to avoid gardening mistakes we have made in the past.

We are good gardeners when we help the God seeds in our fellow gardeners flourish and grow to maturity. But we are not good gardeners if while helping one another's gardens grow; we neglect to care for the original garden of God's creation.

We are to *till* and *keep* the garden... not use and abuse it. If we do not care for creation then creation will not care for us. To ignore our responsibilities to care for the earth is not just a foolish and shortsighted thing to do, it is a blatant affront to God's original intention for our lives. Today our decisions and actions take on global importance as our human footprint covers more and more of the earth. If Christians are to be true to God's original purpose for humanity, then it is Christians who should be on the forefront of efforts to care for this garden we call Earth. Followers on the trail of Jesus are gardeners.

41 - Restoration

I have been known to frequent a local gym. In this gym they maintain a rather large cardboard box in which the items people have left behind or lost are placed in case the owner comes back looking for that stray glove, jacket, or t-shirt etc. It is a lonely place; a place for forgotten things; things whose importance was such that their owner was not mindful of their absence.

The local animal shelter is this kind of a lonely place. Pets that get separated from their owners for whatever reason are confined in a cage until their owner can come and pay the fine to gain their release. If you have ever visited an animal shelter, you know what happens the second you walk into the room where the dogs are contained; you are greeted with an almost overwhelming cacophony of barks and yelps, all of which seem to voice the question that is on all of the captives minds: "Is it you? Is it you? Did you come for me?" Sometimes, the answer to these queries is "Yes. It's me. Let's get you out of here." But, this is not the scenario many of the animals contained at the shelter face, for those whose owners do not come for them or can not be placed with a suitable new owner face a rather dismal outcome, a future not of their choosing…not the future for which they were created.

Restoration is the act of returning something to its rightful owner, returning something to its proper place, or returning something to its original condition.

In our pre-Christian condition, we were in a situation similar to the animals who find themselves in the shelter. We wandered away from our home and our wanderings led us to a place of captivity where we faced a rather bleak future. However, our creator came looking for us, paid the price, and restored us to the family...restored us to the life for which we were created.

Now, having been restored, we too are in the restoration business as we reach out to those who find themselves held captive...held captive to poverty, homelessness, hunger, addiction, loss of hope, despair etc. As followers on the trail of Jesus, we are to join him in restoring these captives to the lives for which they were created...lives in which they are freed from the cages that contain them... lives in which they too can join us in the restoration of everyone and everything in God's creation.

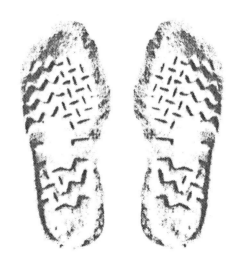

42 - Joy

Joy finds its expression in elation, rejoicing, exultation, jubilation, shouting, and yes...sometimes even dancing. Most often we see joy made visible at sporting events or concerts as individuals whoop and holler and flail about expressing their joy. In church however, such unbridled manifestations of joy are rarely observed outside of a few rather exuberant denominations.

Typically, Christian expressions of joy are much more subdued, reflecting what might be considered a controlled joy so we don't look like some sort of fanatic or crazy person. These muted expressions of Christian joy however lie in contrast to the joy of King David described in 2 Samuel.

In this story, after a period of time in which the Ark of the Covenant was held captive by the Philistines, David was bringing the Ark back home. As King David walked in the processional parade surrounding the Ark, the Bible says David *"danced with great abandon before God."*[134]

Not everyone was enthusiastic at seeing David behave in such a manner. Michal, the daughter of Saul, looked out her window and upon seeing the joy with which David danced *"her heart was filled with scorn."*[135] Later, she expressed her disapproval to the king.

""How wonderfully the king has distinguished himself today - exposing himself to the eyes of the servants' maids like some burlesque street dancer!" David replied to Michal, "In God's presence I'll dance all I want! He chose me over your father and the rest of our family and made me prince over God's

---

[134] 1 Sam 6:14 (The Message)
[135] 2 Sam 6:16, (The Message)

people, over Israel. Oh yes, I'll dance to God's glory more recklessly even than this. And as far as I'm concerned . . . I'll gladly look like a fool."[136]

As if to underscore David's willingness to appear foolish in front of others in his praise of God, he seemingly taunts Michal by saying... you think that was foolish, I can and will be more reckless than that in my celebration of God's goodness. We can almost imagine him breaking into a few gyrations then and there as if to underscore his statement.

As Christians, our joy should not be timid or subdued, but instead we should follow David's example, making our joy visible not only on our faces, but also in our actions. Followers on the trail of Jesus should be easy to spot, they will be the ones gladly looking like fools in joyful celebration of their Lord.

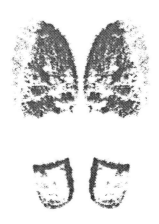

---

[136] 2 Samuel 6:20-22 (The Message)

43 - Incarnation

Incarnation means "the act of assuming flesh."[137] In Christianity, the incarnation refers to our understanding of Jesus as the incarnation of God...God in the flesh. Today, it is easy for us to take this as a given since most, if not all debate on the topic has ceased. However, in the development of the early Church, the incarnation was quite controversial.

Was Jesus a man who God adopted as his son? Did Christ incarnate Jesus at baptism? Did Christ temporarily incarnate the body of Jesus only to depart during the crucifixion since God could not be killed? Or, as Arius argued: "Since the Son was begotten by the Father, He must have been a distinct being and that there must have been (a time) when the Son was not. In other words, He was a creature."[138]

In an effort to avoid what seemed to be the certain fracturing of the Church over this issue, a council of Bishops gathered together in Nicea in 325 C.E. We know the result of their efforts today as the Nicene Creed. With the Nicene Creed, the following language was added as a way to settle the discussion:

We believe in one Lord, Jesus Christ,

the only Son of God,

eternally begotten of the Father,

God from God, Light from Light,

True God from True God,

---

[137] Merrill F. Unger, *The New Unger's Bible Dictionary*, rev. and updated ed. (Chicago: Moody Press, 1988), 613.
[138] Bromiley, *Vol. 4*, 782.

begotten, not made,

of one being with the Father;

through Him all things were made.

"Of one being with the Father." This language underscores and clarifies a fully human and fully divine Jesus. The Bishops agreed that for Jesus to save mankind, Jesus had to be God. They also maintained Jesus had to be fully human for he could not save that which he wasn't. All this to say, much effort has been put into the understanding of Jesus as both fully human and fully divine...the incarnation.

The important thing to remember is this incarnation changes the course of history as an all-powerful God reaches out to embrace his creation. Without it, Christianity is simply one of many belief systems struggling for preeminence in the marketplace of ideas. With it, we have an event without precedence that demands our attention and provides the hope of mankind. The incarnation makes our journey as Jesus followers possible.

44 - Eternal

As humans; we are temporal; we are trapped in time. Up until fairly recent history, humanity lived their lives linked to the passing of the day and the seasons; a gentle rhythm of predictable pace. However, our lives are now ruled by the cruel taskmaster; the clock as modernity has affixed us to the 24 hours, the 1440 minutes, the 86,400 seconds of our day...each of which demand our attention. To make proper use of these units of time, we need to manage them appropriately through strict adherence to our schedules. We arise at certain times. We eat at certain times. We work at certain times. We meet at certain times. The clock is the unforgiving overlord of our existence. As such, coming to grips with the concept of eternal proves challenging, unless of course the routine of your day makes each ticking second seem like an eternity.

Something is eternal when it is without beginning or end. Everything in our physical life experience has a beginning and an end, a rhythm, a cycle to its existence...not so with the eternal. Something eternal is always there. It has been. It is. It will be. This raises a question. If something is always there, does it change? How would it change, because change happens over time and something that is eternal is beyond time? There is no time for eternity.

God's kingdom is an eternal kingdom. When we become followers on the trail of Jesus, we step into that eternal kingdom. Jesus tells us: *"Very truly, I tell you, anyone who hears my word and believes him who sent me has eternal life, and does not come under judgment, but has passed from death to life."*[139]

---

[139] John 5:24

As Christians, we have left the world of the temporal or the temporary and are now citizens of a new world... a world of the living... a world of the eternal.

However, this transition comes with a catch. While we are in fact citizens of this new eternal kingdom, for an undetermined period of time, we continue to be linked to the nature of this earth... its rhythms, its cycles, its seasons of life. In this we maintain a kind of dual citizenship: allegiances to both the temporal and eternal.

Paul gives us some insight into how we should approach this life of coexistence. *"Do not be conformed to this world, but be transformed by the renewing of your minds, so that you may discern what is the will of God—what is good and acceptable and perfect."*[140] The Lord's Prayer contains a phrase that can add clarity as to how we should live this out. In the prayer it says: *"your kingdom come, your will be done on earth as it is in heaven."*[141] Our calling is to enact God's will on earth as it is in heaven. In other words, to be about eternal things in this temporary existence.

As followers of Jesus, we should remain sensitive to the signs of the times in which we live, but first and foremost, keep our gaze affixed to eternity's horizon.

---

[140] Romans 12:2
[141] Matthew 6:10 (NIV)

45 - Emptied

Anyone who has ever driven a car has likely experienced that panicky moment when the low fuel light comes on. If you have, you know this is not a happy time. My worst experience with this was several years ago while driving to Dallas. As most of my driving is typically in town, I had gotten a little lax with paying attention to the fuel gauge. And, on this particular trip, the low fuel light came on about 24 miles from our destination. Unfortunately, our trip meter showed we had 21 miles of fuel left in the car.

In moments like these, anxiety levels tend to rise and continue to increase until we can find a place to get some gas. With each exit we passed, the situation grew more desperate and the anxiety level increased proportionally. Ultimately, we did not find gas that night. But we did not run out of gas. The trip meter had underestimated how far our existing fuel would carry us, allowing us to arrive safely at our destination. Gas was found the next morning. This has not happened again.

Emptiness is a condition we also try to steer clear of on the highway of life. To accomplish this, we fill our lives with any number of things to avoid becoming empty. These emptiness avoidance strategies can manifest in many ways. Sometimes we dodge emptiness by directing our attention toward seemingly harmless distractions, staying busy whenever and on whatever will help keep our life meter from approaching empty; social media is good for this. Or, emptiness avoidance strategies might take the form of behaviors that ultimately end up doing damage to us physically, mentally, or spiritually; activities that seemingly entertain us or help us avoid that empty feeling. Unfortunately, these activities end up being like an uninvited houseguest, consuming our energies and resources only to leave us feeling emptier than we were before.

But, before we give empty a bad rap, there can be an upside to empty. Things must be emptied so that they can be filled.

As followers of Jesus we are called to be...

...emptied of judgment so that we can be filled with forgiveness.

...emptied of hate so that we can be filled with love.

...emptied of deceit so that we can be filled with truth.

...emptied of pride so that we can be filled with gratitude.

In this sense, being emptied is not something that should cause us concern or anxiety. Instead, followers of Jesus should be in a constant process of being emptied, emptied so we can be filled with the things of God.

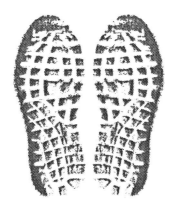

46 - Called/Call

The creation story tells us that after God created the animals, He let Adam do the naming. Or in other words, Adam got to decide what the animals were called...the name by which they would be known.

In our lives, naming rights typically find expression in the naming of our children, or perhaps a pet or two. The sometimes angst filled process of naming a child eventually produces a name that is selected for a variety of reasons including originality, family tradition, or mere happenstance.

However, in Bible times, names were much more than exercises in creativity. They oftentimes revealed something about the person's character, their personality, or even their destiny.[142] For example, when God gave Abraham the news that he and Sarah would have a son in their old age, Abraham fell to the floor laughing.[143] As a result, their son was named *Isaac*, which means *laughter*.[144] And, later when Isaac and Rebekah had two sons, the first was named Esau (which means *hairy*)[145] because he was covered in reddish hair when he was born. And, the second was named Jacob (which means *following after*)[146] because he came out of the womb gripping Esau's heel.[147] These names provided insight into the story of their lives. If we followed a similar trajectory in the naming of children today we can only imagine the catalog of names: Tweet, Text, Post, Gamer, CUL8R etc.

---

[142] Bromiley, *Vol. 3*, 481.

[143] Genesis 17:17

[144] Robert Young, *Young's Analytical Concordance to the Bible* (Peabody: Hendrickson Publishers 01/01/, 2005), 520.

[145] Ibid., 306.

[146] Ibid., 531.

[147] Genesis 25:26

The Bible also tells of how names were oftentimes changed when an individual received a new identity or calling. For example, when God called Abram to become the father of a "multitude of nations",[148] God changed Abram's name to Abraham reflecting a shift from *lofty father* to *multitudinous father*.[149] After an all night wrestling match, Jacob's name (following after) was also changed to Israel (ruling with God)[150] because he has wrestled with God and humans and had prevailed.[151] For Abraham, Israel and others, what they were called (the name by which they were known) was changed to better reflect their calling (what they were called to become).

This re-naming or re-calling continues in the New Testament. John tells of Simon's first encounter with Jesus in which Jesus immediately changes Simon's name. Jesus looked at him and said, ""*You are Simon son of John. You are to be called Cephas" (which is translated Peter).*""[152] Cephas is the Aramaic word for "rock." It is not hard to imagine Simon as somewhat taken aback by this event...curious as to the meaning of this rather strange introduction. The awkwardness of the encounter must have quickly dissipated, for at that moment, Simon the fisherman became Peter...a disciple of Jesus.

As Jesus traveled, taught, and healed, there were many rumors concerning his identity. Jesus asked the disciples what the people were calling Him. The disciples responded: "*Some say John the Baptist, but others Elijah, and still others Jeremiah or one of the prophets.*"[153] But then Jesus asked: "*But who do you say that I am?*"[154] In other words... *what do you call me?* Peter answered,

---

[148] Genesis 17:5
[149] Bromiley, *Vol. 3*, 386.
[150] Young, *Young's Analytical Concordance to the Bible*, 522.
[151] Genesis 32:28
[152] John 1:42
[153] Matthew 16:14
[154] Matthew 16:15

"You are the Messiah, the Son of the living God."[155] Jesus responded, *"Blessed are you, Simon son of Jonah! For flesh and blood has not revealed this to you, but my Father in heaven. And I tell you, you are Peter, and on this rock I will build my church."*[156]

A casual reading does not reveal the depth of meaning contained beneath the surface of this story. But, if we pause here for a moment, a question arises: why did Jesus begin his statement referring to Simon as *Simon son of Jonah* and then in the next sentence call him *Peter*? For the answer, we must return to the initial meeting of Simon and Jesus.

In their first meeting, Simon came face to face with the one his brother Andrew had claimed was the Messiah. In this second encounter, Peter acknowledges Jesus as *the Messiah, the Son of the Living God...*a transformation has occurred in Peter. His transition from Simon to Peter has been fulfilled in his revelation of Jesus as Messiah. Jesus underscores this event by first calling him Simon and then Peter as if to somehow remind everyone of who Peter was and who he had now become. Jesus then states *"And I tell you, you are Peter, and on this rock I will build my church."*[157] Is Peter the rock that will serve as the foundation of the Church because of Peter's physical stature or rock solid immovable faith? This is not likely, since Peter later denied even knowing Jesus when confronted by one of the Chief Priest's servant girls.[158] So, the foundational rock upon which Jesus will build his church can be seen as Peter's revelation or acknowledgement that Jesus is *the Messiah, the Son of the Living God.*

---

[155] Matthew 16:16
[156] Matthew 16:17-18
[157] Matthew 16:18
[158] Mark 14:67-72

Just like Peter, our introduction to Jesus is oftentimes accompanied with confusion or perhaps even a reluctance to accept the reality of who stands before us. But, when we acknowledge and embrace Jesus as the Messiah, the Son of the Living God, we become a new person...we take on a new identity...and this new identity rests upon that foundational rock of revelation that Jesus is indeed the Son of God.

Christians on the trail of Jesus are those who have been called by a new name, a name that unites us on our journey. We are called sons and daughters of the Living God.

47 - Trust

While the word trust has only 5 letters, it's a very big word with very big implications. Relationships, friendships, marriages, contracts, commerce, and even culture are all enabled by trust. Trust is easy when things are going well or when we think we have control over the situation. Trust can be slightly more difficult when we have lost or are losing control.

Trust in God can follow a similar trajectory. It is easy to trust God with our finances when we have money in the bank. It is easy to trust God with our health when there are no ailments threatening our existence. And it is easy to trust God with our futures when the future seems safe and secure. However, it can be challenging to trust God when things are not going so well... when our checking account is running on fumes, when the outcome of the diagnosis is bleak, or when the path we must walk is anything but safe and secure. It is in these situations we tend to find out if we truly trust God or if our trust has been in our own ability to seemingly control our destiny.

The Bible tells many stories of trust... trust earned, trust lost, trust betrayed. One story in which the prime characters must trust when the elements of the story seem to indicate a less than desirable outcome, is the story of Shadrach, Meshach, and Abednego.

In the story, Daniel had become a member of King Nebuchadnezzar's court. His position of privilege allowed him to appoint three fellow Hebrews (Shadrach, Meshach, and Abednego) to positions of authority in Nebuchadnezzar's court as well. As the story goes, Nebuchadnezzar had a golden statue built and commanded all his government officials to bow down and worship the statue. Not bowing down to this statue would result in being thrown into a blazing furnace.

Those who were possibly jealous of Shadrach, Meshach and Abednego's newly found position of influence reported to King Nebuchadnezzar that these Hebrews were not participating in the ceremony. The King had them brought before him to answer for their recalcitrance. In their defense, Shadrach, Meshach and Abednego made the following statement: *"If our God whom we serve is able to deliver us from the furnace of blazing fire and out of your hand, O king, let him deliver us. But if not, be it known to you, O king, that we will not serve your gods and we will not worship the golden statue that you have set up."*[159]

Shadrach, Meshach, and Abednego expressed their hope that God would rescue them from the fiery furnace. But, and this is a big but, they also trusted God to be with them in case rescue was not forthcoming. Shadrach, Meshach, and Abednego were indeed thrown into a fire so hot that those who threw them in were killed by its heat. However, God protected all three of them from the fire and they exited unharmed. As a result, King Nebuchadnezzar made it illegal to speak against the God of Shadrach, Meshach, and Abednego.

The story ended well, but it could just as easily gone the other way. We could have been reading a story of three men who were martyred for their allegiance to God. Religious history is full of many such stories. Stories of those whose trust in the Lord went without visible reward in this world. But in the Kingdom of God, this trust does not go unrewarded. As followers on the path of Jesus, we have learned or are in the process of learning that our only

---

[159] Daniel 3:17-18

hope is to trust the Lord. And, if we have faith like Shadrach, Meshach, and Abednego, this trust will not go up in smoke.

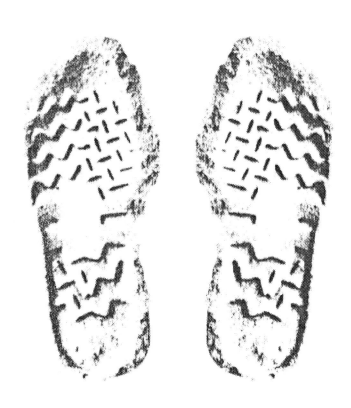

48 - Prayer

Most of us have friends. These friendships typically vary across a wide spectrum of closeness. We have friends we see often; those whose presence is a reassuring part of our lives. We have friends that maybe we should more accurately call acquaintances; those we speak to or acknowledge in public but never spend time with. And then there are those friends who when they contact us, we know they are doing so because they need something. Very little has been invested into this type of relationship, but when they need something, you are the one they lean on for assistance.

Prayer is a part of our relationship with God. Some of us feel very close to God in that we spend a lot of time together in prayer. God's presence is a reassuring part of our lives. Others of us are not really friends with God but we are acquainted, acknowledging God's presence at church but never really investing the time to get to know God. And then there are those of us who invest very little into our relationship with God, only calling upon him when our needs exceed our capacities.

Relationships are strengthened as we spend time together. We talk, we tell stories, and we listen. Over time, this is how we get to know one another.

Prayer is the way our relationship with God is strengthened. We talk, we tell stories, and we listen. Over time, prayer is how we get to know God.

Followers of Jesus are prayers.

49 - Disciple

The Greek word in the New Testament we know as the word "disciple" is the word μαθητής or mathetes. It means *learner*[160] or *taught or trained one.*[161] The New Testament commonly uses the term "disciple" to refer to those members of Jesus' group who he chose to accompany him in life and ministry. As disciples, they were *learners*...those being *taught or trained* in the ways of Jesus.

One thing that we can learn from the story of Jesus and his disciples is that discipleship occurs over a period of time...in this case three years. During these three years the disciples journeyed with Jesus, they observed and were taught the basics of what it means to a disciple of Jesus. Many times the path was difficult and confusing, but with patience and practice they picked up the rhythms of this new life. When Jesus was crucified and buried, they no doubt felt confused and disoriented, afraid that without their teacher they were lost...unprepared for what lay ahead of them.

But, Jesus did not leave them in this confused condition very long. He soon appeared to them alive and gave them a mission. Jesus told them, *"All authority in heaven and on earth has been given to me. Go therefore and make disciples of all nations, baptizing them in the name of the Father and of the Son and of the Holy Spirit, and teaching them to obey everything that I have commanded you."*[162] They were given a mission to not only baptize and teach - they were given a mission to make disciples. They were now the teachers.

---

[160] http://concordances.org/greek/3101.htm
[161] Young, *Young's Analytical Concordance to the Bible*, 257.
[162] Matthew 28:18-20

The challenges associated with this mission would no doubt have seemed overwhelming were it not for the next statement, *"And remember, I am with you always, to the end of the age."*[163] Jesus may have been about to leave them in physical form but would always remain with them via the spirit… the Holy Spirit. He said: *"And I will ask the Father, and he will give you another Advocate, to be with you forever. This is the Spirit of truth, whom the world cannot receive, because it neither sees him nor knows him. You know him, because he abides with you, and he will be in you."*[164] While they were the new teachers, their period of learning and training was not over. The teacher was not done. The Holy Spirit would continue to teach, inform, and accompany them on every step of their journey.

Today, as followers and disciples on the trail of Jesus, we are also on the journey of learning how to walk with and live in the ways of Jesus. But, we are not just students of an ancient text that instructs us with a better way of life. As disciples, we too have the Holy Spirit within us to comfort, teach, and inspire as we set out to do the work Jesus gave us… the work of being his disciples.

---

[163] Matthew 28:20
[164] John 14:16-17

50 - Real

How you doin' man?

Great, how are you doin'?

Great...great...

How's your wife (husband) and kids?

Just doing great... how are yours?

Good too.

Well, good to see you.

You too.

Let's do lunch sometime soon.

Sounds good. Text me.

Real or fake? Fake...right? But this is how many of our social interactions go...even in church...maybe especially in church. Not being perfect is seen in some circles as not having enough faith. So to admit there is an issue or maybe multiple issues in our lives would reveal our realness...it would reveal that we are less than perfect. Being real comes with consequences. Real is the opposite of fake. Real is authentic.

Jesus is real. The story of Jesus in the Bible is real. In the writings of the disciples, they were not afraid to reveal the realness of Jesus. Jesus got mad, got tired, ripped some people a new one, prayed for strength, and contemplated the possibility of his not having to go through with the crucifixion...that is real.

The disciples were real too. They doubted, they questioned, they jockeyed for position, they were confused, one betrayed Jesus, and at the moment when Jesus was most vulnerable, they ran for their lives. They no doubt questioned their experience and what it all meant as they gathered to discuss what to do in light of the death of their Messiah.

But then something real happened. After his crucifixion and burial, Jesus appeared alive to the disciples in all his realness. As we discussed earlier for signpost #9-Fellowship, the disciple Thomas was not among them when this happened and upon hearing the news Thomas expressed his doubts. He said: *"Unless I see the mark of the nails in his hands, and put my finger in the mark of the nails and my hand in his side, I will not believe."*[165] In other words, unless I see Jesus in the flesh, unless I see the real scars in his real body...the real Jesus, I will not believe.

When Jesus appeared again to the disciples a week later, Thomas was in attendance. After greeting the others, Jesus looked directly at Thomas and said *"Put your finger here and see my hands. Reach out your hand and put it in my side. Do not doubt but believe."*[166] Thomas answered him: *"My Lord and my God!"*[167] When confronted with the real Jesus...the scars proved the realness of the resurrection, Thomas was without doubt.

Many of our friends and family are doubtful of our faith. They have heard the stories. They have heard the impassioned pleas of those concerned with their eternal destiny. They have heard it all before, and yet they remain doubtful, skeptical, and possibly even hostile to the message of Christ. What they need is something real. They need to see people who are living out their

---

[165] John 20:25
[166] John 20:27
[167] John 20:28

faith while being unashamed of their scars...their realness. Thomas would not believe until he saw Jesus' scars. Likely, many of those around us are like Thomas. They will not believe unless they see our scars...scars that can help them believe we are real...scars that provide evidence of our healing, scars that point them toward Jesus as the healer of their wounds.

Followers on the trail of Jesus serve a real Lord and Savior. As such, we owe him nothing less than to be real with our fellow disciples and friends, for it is in this realness we will provide evidence to the realness of our Lord.

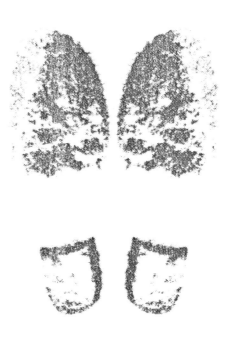

51 - Generosity/Generous

It is typically much easier to be generous out of our abundance rather that to engage in giving that is sacrificial...giving that is going to cost us something. If I have enough money to buy my lunch and your lunch, you are much more likely to get a free lunch than if I only have enough money for one lunch...just saying. But most of us are that way. We embrace the idea of giving out of our excess or abundance, but typically find ourselves less than generous when abundance is a word not associated with our current situation.

In contrast, the Gospel is about a generosity that came with great personal cost...a sacrificial generosity. Paul reminds us we did nothing to earn our salvation, but instead it was a generous gift.

"Since all have sinned and fall short of the glory of God; they are now justified by his grace as a gift, through the redemption that is in Christ Jesus."[168]

This was no free lunch. Jesus didn't just give out of his abundance, Jesus gave it all. As a result, we find ourselves the recipients of an abundant grace beyond anything we deserve or can ever hope to repay.

Luke 12:38 tells us that *"Great gifts mean great responsibilities; greater gifts, greater responsibilities!"* What greater gift than the gift of our forgiveness and redemption through Jesus' gift? What greater responsibility than to share this gift with others?

In light of the great enormity of this gift, the only way we can ease its burden is to be generous with others. This generosity should be counted as privilege as our giving finds its source in the abundant and endless resources

---

[168] Romans 3:23-24

of God rather than in the limits of our personal ability. As followers on the trail of Jesus, our generosity is out of abundance…the abundance of God.

52 - Transparent

In ancient cultures, when a city fell on hard times or was destroyed; rather than removing the debris, the city was re-built on top of the rubble. Over the centuries, this cycle could repeat itself time and time again causing the city to gradually rise in elevation. The mounds that would result from this process are called *tells*. Archeological excavation of these *tells* serves to uncover the truth of civilizations buried beneath the surface for centuries.

Interestingly, the game of poker also has something called a *tell*. I am told, to be a good poker player one must have a good poker face. A good poker face is one that reveals nothing. Anything that reveals the truth of your cards or your intentions is called a *tell*. A *tell* might be a twitch, a scratch on the nose, or the way you hold your cards when you are bluffing. Poker players work to minimize or eliminate any action that could reveal their intentions because a *tell* can cause you to lose the game.

In each of these examples, the word *tell* refers to something that is hidden or concealed which is the opposite of our word *transparent*.

As Christians, we should not be about burying the debris of our lives beneath layer upon layer of public persona, leaving the truth of our stories to be uncovered by only the most persistent of excavators.

Likewise, the reason for our behavior and actions should not be hidden behind an exterior that is impossible to read, leaving people to second guess our true intentions.

Instead, everything we do and say should be a *tell*...a clue or a sign that points to the reason for our existence...to our Jesus. The scars of our lives should serve to *tell* our story of redemption while our actions should serve to reveal the one who inspires our imaginations. The more transparent followers on the trail of Jesus become, the more Jesus will be revealed to others searching for the trail. This is good news, good news we should not be ashamed to tell.

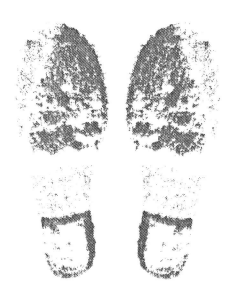

53 - Transformation

Makeover shows are very popular on television. These shows tell the story of a person who for some reason is tired of the way they look and agree to allow a group of experts to completely remake their appearance. The show typically tracks the advice, the shopping trips, the haircut, and the application of make-up which all lead up to the dramatic revealing of the new look. While the change is oftentimes dramatic and seems to somehow provide the person with a fresh outlook on what their life can now become, eventually hair will grow, fashions will fade, and looks will change.

Makeovers can indeed be radical transformations. However, they pale in comparison to the transformation that occurs in us when we become a follower of Jesus Christ. Paul clarifies the extent of the Christian transformation for us.

"I have been crucified with Christ. My ego is no longer central. It is no longer important that I appear righteous before you or have your good opinion, and I am no longer driven to impress God. Christ lives in me. The life you see me living is not 'mine,' but it is lived by faith in the Son of God, who loved me and gave himself for me."[169]

Paul's old self, like our old self...the self that was concerned with appearances... the self whose identity was dependent on the opinion of others...the self that tried to appear good enough for God... that self was crucified on the cross along with Jesus. As a result, we become a new creation in Christ. New clothes, new hair, and new make-up can indeed change the

---

[169] Galatians 2:20 (The Message)

appearance of followers on the trail of Jesus, but it is Jesus himself who brings about the most radical transformation in our lives.

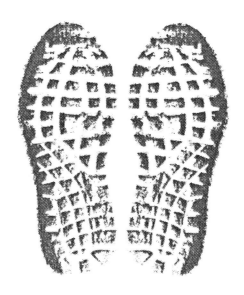

54 - Surrender

When flipping through the television channels in hopes of finding something to watch, it is oftentimes tempting to pause for a moment when we stumble upon one of those extreme cage-fighting events. If you linger on the channel very long, you will likely learn that the fighters can tap out or surrender when they want the match to stop. They tap out by tapping the body of their opponent in hopes of putting an end to their suffering. The point at which a fighter taps out indicates the level of pain they can tolerate as they attempt to defeat their adversary. Tapping out is typically something to be avoided in these matches because when you tap out, you lose the match. As such, it appears that the wrestlers only tap out if they are in danger of physical injury or worse.

Many of us are similar to these wrestlers when it comes to surrendering to God. We do our best to wrestle with whatever life throws at us in an attempt to win on our own. In many instances, we only tap out or surrender to God when the circumstances take such a drastic turn for the worse that we are left with no where else to turn. Desperate circumstances require desperate actions and sometimes this results in a desperate crying out for God to intervene. We tap out in hopes that God will tap in.

We may try to tap out when driving home after too many hours in front of the tap finds us at the side of the road attempting a sobriety test. We may try to tap out when waiting on the results of the home pregnancy test we hope reveals a preferred outcome. We may try to tap out when any number of human failings finds us at the end of our abilities.

Followers on the trail of Jesus are those who have surrendered and continue to surrender… those who have tapped out…those who have abandoned the desire to do it on their own in exchange for the ability to join with a God who can do all things.

55 - Steadfast

Steadfast means "firmly fixed in faith or devotion to duty; constant; unchanging."[170] The Pharisees and Sadducees were steadfast. As a minority people, in a seemingly hostile environment, their steadfastness provided comfort as a constant, unchanging presence in the lives of the Jewish people. No one would question their devotion to the rituals and traditions, as they were staunch defenders and sometimes enforcers of proper practices of the faith. Ironically, it was this steadfastness that blinded them, leaving them unable to recognize Jesus as God in their midst.

As followers of Jesus today, it is easy to view our situation from a similar perspective as we too live in a culture that is increasingly hostile to Christianity, challenging our faith at most every turn. This situation might tempt us to react much in the same way the Pharisees and Sadducees did, defending our practices and traditions as the glue that holds us together. However, our call is not to remain steadfast in this regard, but to remain steadfast to Jesus and his mission. Jesus told us: *"I came that they may have life, and have it abundantly."*[171] This is the lens through which our traditions and practices should be evaluated and the soil in which they are encouraged to prosper and grow.

Traditions and practices may change, as the Pharisees and Sadducees found out, but the mission will always be the same. As followers on the trail of Jesus we are called to be steadfast, steadfast to the mission of Jesus

---

170 Funk & Wagnalls, 1226.
171 John 10:10 NRSV

56 - Sojourner

A sojourn is a temporary stay. Therefore a sojourner is a visitor, a temporary resident, someone who is on the go, away from his or her home.

At home we are in familiar surroundings. We have things they way we like them. Typically we feel safe and secure. We know where things are and how to get from place to place. We know the climate and can prepare properly for the day.

But when we travel, we find ourselves in unfamiliar surroundings. Things may not be the way we like them. We may not feel safe and secure. We may not know how to get from place to place. We may not know the climate, leaving us unprepared for what nature offers us.

All of this can be disconcerting; making the sojourner wish they were at home. In light of this, Peter gives us a bit of bad news.

"Friends, this world is not your home, so don't make yourselves cozy in it."[172]

So, when the news of the day makes us feel less than secure, when the rate of change leaves us unsettled in unfamiliar territory, when the social climate we find ourselves in makes us feel unprepared for what awaits us, Peter reminds us: this world is not our home.

Followers of Jesus are sojourners, visitors, temporary residents in this world: those who are away from, but on their way home.

---

[172] 1 Peter 2:11 MSG

57 - Salt

"You are the salt of the earth; but if salt has lost its taste, how can its saltiness be restored? It is no longer good for anything, but is thrown out and trampled under foot."[173]

Most of us are familiar with the common explanations given for the use of the word salt in this scripture and how it relates to Christian life.

• Just as salt tends to bring out the flavor of food, Christians are to bring out the flavors life…to help bring meaning and joy where it is hard to find.

• Just as salt acts as a preservative for food, Christians are those who enact the eternal concerns of God on this earth; the preservers of eternal truths.

These are good and proper, but lets go a little deeper. The Hebrew Bible includes the following references to salt (among others):

"You shall not omit from your grain offerings the salt of the covenant with your God; with all your offerings you shall offer salt."[174]

"All the holy offerings that the Israelites present to the Lord I have given to you, together with your sons and daughters, as a perpetual due; it is a covenant of salt forever before the Lord for you and your descendants as well."[175]

"Do you not know that the Lord God of Israel gave the kingship over Israel forever to David and his sons by a covenant of salt?"[176]

---

[173] Matthew 5:13
[174] Leviticus 2:13
[175] Numbers 18:19
[176] 2 Chronicles 13:5

Salt in this sense is a covenantal symbol suggesting Gods covenants are "fixed, permanent, and unchangeable, enduring forever."[177]

Interestingly, when a child was born in Bible times, they were given a bath and were rubbed with salt before being wrapped with a blanket.[178] Apart from any medicinal purposes, this practice endured for symbolic reasons; connecting newborn children to the enduring covenants of God.

Salt is also absolutely necessary for the proper functioning of our bodies. A low salt level, brought about by exercise or heat can result in a condition known as hyponatremia.[179] Symptoms include "nausea, muscle cramps, disorientation, slurred speech, confusion, and inappropriate behavior."[180] In extreme cases, salt depletion can induce a coma or even death.

When we allow these additional insights to better inform our understanding of Jesus' statement *"You are the salt of the earth"*[181] we see followers of Jesus:

- Bring out the flavors of life

- Act as a preservative to the eternal truths of God

- Are a people of the covenant

- Contribute to the proper functioning of the Body of Christ

Followers on the trail of Jesus are a salty bunch.

---

[177] H. Clay Trumball, *The Covenant of Salt* (New York: Charles Scribner's Sons, 1899), 142.
[178] Bromiley, *Vol. 4*, 286.
[179] http://www.rice.edu/~jenky/sports/salt.html
[180] Ibid.
[181] Matthew 5:13

58 - Saints

Anyone that has ever had to close the estate of a relative knows the angst involved with deciding what to keep, what to sell, and what to give away for each item seems bring back a memory or a story we want to hold on to... but we can't keep it all. So, we go through a process of picking out those things that have a special meaning for us above the others. This meaning could be associated with a season of life or an event. Or, it could be an item that seems to reflect the essence of who someone was or what it was like to live in a particular place. As we go through these items we set-apart the keepers from the rest of the inventory.

I have several "keepers" strategically placed in my office. A chrome-plated jigger sits on my bookshelf as a remembrance of my Great Aunt Margie. Each day after work in the shoe factory, she would come home and make herself a highball using that jigger. Looking at that little metal icon brings back memories of her...of her love of fun, fishing, playing cards, great food, and hunting for morels in the woods of Missouri.

On my desk I also have two small well-used pocketknives; one belonged to my grandfather and the other to my father. My grandfather used his pocketknife to set the pace for the opening of Christmas presents among other things. The energy of children anxious to get on with it was always brought back into line by the very deliberate and methodical slices that knife slowly made on the tape holding the paper to the package. One look at that knife and I am a kid, sitting on the floor waiting for my turn to open Christmas presents.

The second knife belonged to my father. Its sole purpose was to clean the carbon out of his corncob pipes to extend their usefulness. A glance at that pocketknife is to be back sitting in the den of my childhood home with the smell of pipe tobacco filling the room.

You too likely have relics from your family history scattered around your home. So what does all this have to do with the word *saints*?

The word *saints* in the Bible is not used in reference to individuals that have long ago gone to be with Jesus or to pay tribute to those whose piety rose above that of common men and women. It is instead used to identify those individuals that are set apart, the separate and holy followers of Jesus.[182] We see this in Paul's greeting to the church in Corinth.

"To the church of God that is in Corinth, to those who are sanctified in Christ Jesus, called to be saints, together with all those who in every place call on the name of our Lord Jesus Christ, both their Lord and ours: Grace to you and peace from God our Father and the Lord Jesus Christ."[183]

As saints, we are not unlike my family artifacts, for we too were rescued from destruction, separated for special meaning, and destined to serve as reminders...not as reminders of days gone by, but as reminders of the future Jesus summons us to embrace.

The final verse of the Bible is a benediction that reminds Jesus' followers of our saintly place in the story.

"The grace of the Lord Jesus be with all the saints. Amen."[184]

...and Amen.

---

[182] Young, *Young's Analytical Concordance to the Bible*, 831.
[183] 1 Corinthians 1:2-3
[184] Revelation 22:21

59 - Generational

A generation refers to a group of people who grow to maturity in a common era. These generations cover a span of about 30 years.[185] We like to assign names to these various generations. We have the Greatest Generation (thank you Tom Brokaw). They were the ones who fought and experienced World War II. We then have the Baby Boomers who are said to think of themselves as a special generation.[186] The Boomers are followed by Generation X - the Baby Busters, Generation Y - the Millennials, Generation Z - the Internet generation, and then what has been called Generation AO - Always On[187] in reference to their constant connection to technology.

Each of these generations has a slightly different outlook on life. Their desires, motivations, and interests etc. are at least partly determined by the era and culture in which they live.

Every generation presents the Church with a unique set of challenges. In response, some are tempted to circle the wagons in defense against what can feel like an all out assault on all things Christian. However, as missionaries in what feels like a foreign land, we must instead, accept the generational challenge, choose to move forward on unfamiliar terrain, learn to communicate in the language of the culture, and build bridges rather than walls, for it is across these bridges followers of Jesus can welcome each generation home.

---

[185] http://oxforddictionaries.com/definition/generation?region=us&q=generation
[186] Doug Owram, *Born at the Right Time: A History of the Baby Boom Generation* (Toronto: University of Toronto Press, Scholarly Publishing Division, 1997), xi.
[187] http://www.elon.edu/e-web/predictions/expertsurveys/2012survey/default.xhtml)

60 - And

Our God is an *and* God. The very substance and nature of God is *and*; singular *and* Trinitarian; Father, Son *and* Holy Spirit. We find this and-ness reflected through scripture.

- After creating Adam, God decided it was not good for man to be alone…enter Adam *and* Eve.

- Since God is the creator of life, those who are made in the image of this creator also get to create life on this earth. Naturally, this act of creation occurs in an *and* relationship…humanity is not created in isolation… it requires a coming together… it requires an *and*.

- Our God is not a distant God who choses to be admired or revealed from afar. Instead, God is revealed in relationship through Jesus who was fully human *and* fully divine.

- Jesus did not live out his life alone on a mountaintop. Jesus chose companions. This group is referred to as Jesus *and* the disciples. When Jesus sent these twelve disciples on a mission trip, he did not send them alone but sent them two by two…[188] one *and* another.

- The Bible tells of Jesus being asked which of the commandments was greatest, which one was the most important… of course it was an *"and"* answer.

"The first is, "Hear, O Israel: the Lord our God, the Lord is one; you shall love the Lord your God with all your heart, and with all your soul, and with all

---

[188] Mark 6:7

your mind, and with all your strength." The second is this, "You shall love your neighbor as yourself." There is no other commandment greater than these."[189]

The first concerns our relationship to God *and* the second concerns our relationship to one another.

As Christians on the trail of Jesus, we can tell if we are on the right path by looking at our *ands*. If we are going it alone, we are on the wrong path.

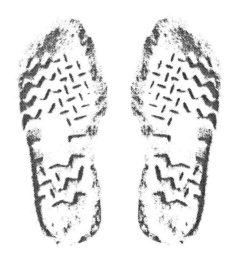

---

[189] Mark 12:29-31

61 - Uncomfortable

Christianity is oftentimes promoted as the antidote to a troubled life or in more illusory presentations, as a life raft on which we can ride safely away from our problems toward more peaceful and calm waters. However, attempts like these to paint a giant happy face on the Gospel are at the least; not scriptural, and at the worst; misleading. C.S. Lewis perhaps said it best: "I didn't go to religion to make me happy. I always knew a bottle of Port would do that. If you want a religion to make you feel really comfortable, I certainly don't recommend Christianity."[190] Those of us who have been at this for a while know, being a Christian comes with a certain amount of uncomfortableness. This is nothing new.

When Jesus first met the disciples, minding their own business, fishing as they likely had done every day for years...what happened? Jesus walked up and asked them to leave the comfort of their routine, their families, their homes, their way of life, and follow Him. Even though the Bible says they dropped their nets and followed, one can guess this made them a little uncomfortable. This was, however, not the most uncomfortable thing they would do, for in their time together, Jesus challenged their thinking, their theology, their place in the world, and even their identity. Uncomfortableness was a way of life for the disciples as they learned to place faithfulness over and above their uncomfortableness.

As followers of Jesus today, he has given us a glimpse of what heaven can look like. But, this too can and should make us uncomfortable: uncomfortable when people are hungry, homeless, hopeless, taken advantage of, used, unloved, racially profiled, dismissed, discarded, left alone, ignored, discriminated against, excluded, denied, trafficked, sold, prostituted, and demeaned to name a few.

Uncomfortableness arises because we know Jesus is standing before us, asking us to follow him into the midst of these problems: to leave the comfort of our routine, sometimes our families, our homes, and our way of life. This call can threaten our theology, our place in the world, and maybe even our identity. But like the disciples of old and generations since have learned: when faithfulness overcomes uncomfortableness, the Kingdom of God is enacted on this earth. Followers of Jesus are called to get comfortable with being uncomfortable.

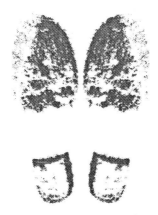

[190] C. S. Lewis, *God in the Dock: Essays On Theology and Ethics* (Grand Rapids, MI: Eerdmans Pub Co, 1994), 58.

62 - Sacrifice

To sacrifice is the act of giving up something that is valued for the sake of something else regarded as more important or worthy.[191] Our culture celebrates stories of sacrifice...the stories of those who disregard their own well being for the sake of someone else. We love to honor and pay tribute to those who seemingly cast aside all concern for themselves to rush into a burning building or dive into a rushing river to rescue individuals they likely did not even know existed just moments before. These stories serve to inspire and remind us of the greatness that lies within.

In return for these acts of sacrifice, those who are rescued oftentimes feel they owe a debt to the rescuer. But, more often than not, the debt is repaid by living life with a renewed appreciation and enthusiasm as the rescued one attempts to help others view the world from the gifted vantage point they now enjoy.

The Bible says, *"Greater love hath no man than this, that a man lay down his life for his friends."*[192] This is the overarching story of the New Testament: Jesus laid down his life to rescue us so that we might have everlasting life. But, how could we ever hope to repay this debt... what could we offer in reasonable exchange for this gift of life? Paul gives us an idea as to how we should approach this dilemma: *"I beseech you therefore, brethren, by the mercies of God, that ye present your bodies a living sacrifice, holy, acceptable unto God, which is your reasonable service."*[193]

---

[191] http://oxforddictionaries.com/definition/sacrifice?region=us&q=sacrifice
[192] John 15:13 (KJV)
[193] Romans 12:1 (KJV)

What is reasonable is that we present our bodies or in other words live our lives as a living sacrifice... to live life as an expression of the love that drew Jesus to the cross.

Each and every day as followers of Jesus we will be tempted to step away from this service and pursue the things that tend to distract us from this calling. But, this living sacrifice is not too difficult to bear. It is merely what is reasonable, as we (the rescued ones) aid in the rescue of others so that they too can experience life from the gifted vantage point we now enjoy.

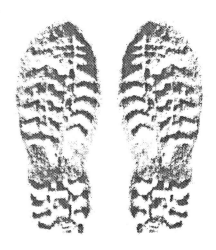

63 - Ekklesia

The word *ekklesia* is the Greek word in the New Testament we know today as the word *church*. It literally means, "that which is called out."[194] It is the root of the Latin word *ecclesia* from which we get the words *ecclesiastical* - things having to do with church, and the word *ecclesiology* - things having to do with church doctrine. However, "during the time of Jesus, the word *ekklesia* was used almost without exception to refer to a political assembly that was regularly convened for the purpose of making decisions."[195]

This raises the question of how a secular word with strong political implications for the time period[196] came to be the primary word used when referring to a gathering of Christians. It is especially interesting since they had an existing lexicon of Greek words to potentially describe a gathering of Jesus' followers, such as *synagogye* (assembly) or *thiasos* (a voluntary association of worshipers) or even *eranos* (an intellectual discussion group).[197]

Here are a couple of things we can learn from Paul's choice of the word *ekklesia* in the New Testament. First, Paul's re-purposing of a familiar word into a Christian context provides us with an important lesson in how we should not hesitate to draw upon the cultural lexicon to more effectively communicate with the culture.

Secondly, the word *ekklesia* serves to remind us of the original vision for our churches as active and participatory faith communities.

---

[194] Young, *Young's Analytical Concordance to the Bible*, 166.

[195] Stephen E. Atkerson, *House Church - Simple-Strategic-Scriptural* (Atlanta: New Testament Reformation Fellowship, 2008), 73.

[196] Ibid.

[197] Ibid.

And so, followers on the trail of Jesus are to be found in active, energetic faith communities; unashamedly re-purposing that which is familiar to the culture in ways that fulfill the ancient purposes of our faith.

Ekklesia…

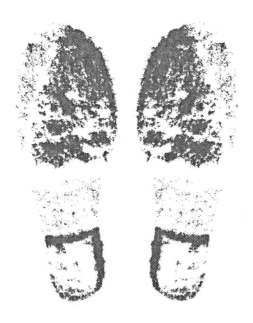

64 - Kindness

For some reason, the Internet seems to bring out the worst in some people as they toss their heated polemic back and forth from behind the firewall of anonymity. People post things on the electronic public square they would never say in public, let alone face-to-face (or at least we hope not).

Christians are, needless to say, not immune from this public display of self-righteousness and insensitivity. Attempts to comment on a particular aspect of someone's theology or position can rapidly slide down the rhetorical slippery slope until it descends to name calling and accusations of heresy. Even if the truth is on your side, an unkind presentation makes the truth much more difficult to receive.

Perhaps this is why an instruction in Micah 6:8 comes with not only a strategy, but also a methodology.

"He has told you, O mortal, what is good; and what does the Lord require of you but to do justice, and to love kindness, and to walk humbly with your God?"

God says it is good to do justice, to stand up for those who cannot stand up for themselves. But for our efforts to be truly good, they must be clothed in kindness and humility.

In kindness, the truth can begin to touch the untouchable, approach the unapproachable, and heal the gaping wounds of those who have chosen to distance themselves from the truth due to unkind words and actions in the past. Followers of Jesus are those who build bridges of kindness across which the truth is free to travel.

65 - Seeking

Many a day growing up was spent playing hide and seek. There is just something fun about that game. Maybe this is because its one of the first games we learn to play or maybe its because it requires no equipment... only willing participants...who knows. But, we know where it starts. It begins when Mommy or Daddy place their faces in front of their baby, cover their face with their hands and say "where's Mommy" or "where's Daddy" only to reveal their smiling faces and say "there she/he is!" At this point in the game, joyous sounds of laughter fill the room.

This game can also work in reverse as the parent pretends not to see the baby only to quickly find it right in front of them. The acknowledgement of the baby's presence once again elicits the joyous laughter of both participants.

Hide and seek does not seem to come with an expiration date since we continue to play it in elementary school and beyond.

As we reach adulthood however, our games of hide and seek get more elaborate as our reasons to hide can outweigh our reasons to seek. At this point, hide and seek is no longer just a game.

One of the first stories in the Bible tells us of Adam and Eve hiding from God. This was not a game however. They hid because they had disobeyed...done the one thing God had forbidden them to do...tasted the forbidden fruit of the Tree of Knowledge and with apple juice still streaming down their cheeks...Adam and Eve hid.

"They heard the sound of the Lord God walking in the garden at the time of the evening breeze, and the man and his wife hid themselves from the

presence of the Lord God among the trees of the garden. But the Lord God called to the man, and said to him, "Where are you?"[198]

This has always been one of the more curious stories in the Bible. When Adam and Eve hear the sound of God walking in the Garden... the all-powerful God...the all-knowing creator of the universe... they hide...as if they could place themselves somewhere beyond the presence of God. And then God (who must enjoy a good game of hide and seek) plays along asking, "Where are you?"...as if he did not know exactly where they were and why they were hiding.

Many of us attempt to play the same game with God? When we find ourselves with the apple juice of disgrace and disobedience on our faces, we attempt to runaway or hide? Before many of us became followers of Jesus, we tried to justify our distance from God by saying we were not good enough or perhaps we felt it necessary to delay that commitment until we could get our act together. Even after becoming followers of Jesus and doing our best to live a Christian life, we oftentimes fail to meet what we think are the accepted standards of behavior and begin to back away from the presence of God. This retreat can manifest itself by not praying, not reading the Bible, or not remaining in fellowship with other Christians. We begin to hide from the presence of God... as if we could.

But, the good news of the story in the garden and the Gospel is that while we may attempt to hide or run away from God out of shame, embarrassment, or outright defiance, God will come looking for us...seeking to bring us back into fellowship.

---

[198] Genesis 3:8-9

God is always seeking his children who are lost or hiding and when God pulls back that which attempts to obscure us from his view...let the joyous laughter that rises from our redemption begin.

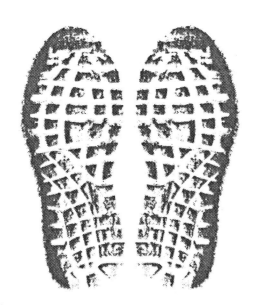

66 - Purity

More than half of the instances of the word "pure" in the Old Testament are in reference to gold.[199] These references begin in Exodus when God gives Moses an assignment to build a sanctuary.[200] Contained within the sanctuary was to be an ark of acacia wood overlaid with *pure* gold, four rings of gold, poles for the ark that are overlaid with gold, a mercy seat of *pure* gold, two cherubim of gold, a table overlaid with *pure* gold, gold plates, gold dishes, gold pitchers, gold bowls, *pure* gold lamp stands etc. *Pure* oil and *pure* frankincense were also required for these utensils.

In Leviticus, God outlined many ritual sacrifices his people must engage in to restore themselves to good standing: to atone for their sins. Leviticus contains reference after reference to the specific type of animal required for these sacrifices. The single trait these animals share is that they are to be without blemish...to be perfect...in other words pure.

Several hundred years later, Solomon built a temple for God. And again, *purity* played a large part in its construction. The interior of the sanctuary was overlaid with *pure* gold; there were to be *pure* gold lamp stands, *pure* gold cups, *pure* gold bowls, *pure* gold dishes etc.

It would have been hard for the nation of Israel to miss the lesson: things which were acceptable to God were to be *pure*, without blemish.

New Testament writer Paul has a bit of an existential crisis over purity concerns.

---

[199] Bromiley, *Vol. 4*, 1054.
[200] Exodus 25ff.

"I realize that I don't have what it takes. I can will it, but I can't do it. I decide to do good, but I don't really do it; I decide not to do bad, but then I do it anyway."[201]

Paul concludes…

"Wretched man that I am! Who will rescue me from this body of death? Thanks be to God through Jesus Christ our Lord!"[202]

Like Paul, we all fall short. We are not fit for the sanctuary. We can never be *pure* enough or good enough to approach the throne room of God in spite of our best intentions. But, as followers of Jesus, God sees us through the *pure* lens of Jesus Christ. It is through his *purity* that we find ourselves able to stand in the presence of God.

---

[201] Romans 7:18-19 (The Message)
[202] Romans 7:24-25

67 - New

Most of us, at least those of us in the West, are pretty into new. New is better right? And if we are going to try to promote a product, the best way to do that is by coming up with some new features, a new formula, new color, or maybe even new packaging, etc.

If anyone mastered the art of selling us new it had to be Steve Jobs. Steve could sell new in ways that caused us to get in line and sleep in tents overnight in front of the store just so we could be the first to have the new one.

In his book The Inevitable, Kevin Kelly tells us "every 12 months we produce 8 million new songs, 2 million new books, 16,000 new films, 30 billion blog posts, 182 billion tweets, 400,000 new products."[203]

We are all about new. Even when we want to change something in our lives we say we turn over a new leaf or tomorrow's a new day.

But we should be about new, shouldn't we? If we are modeled in the image of the Creator, we should be all about creating...creating something new.

It would appear Paul was also kind of into new.

"So if anyone is in Christ, there is a new creation: everything old has passed away; see, everything has become new!"[204]

Paul understood the depth of newness brought about by Jesus. Paul had been a Pharisee from a long line of Pharisees...[205] a persecutor of the Church

---

[203] Kevin Kelly, *The Inevitable: Understanding the 12 Technological Forces That Will Shape Our Future* (New York, New York: Viking, 2016), 165.
[204] 2 Corinthians 5:17 (NRSV)

who was previously on a mission to destroy this new Jesus sect and its followers. Paul did not like this new thing. But something new happened in Paul. He was transformed in dramatic fashion into something new and baptized shortly thereafter. He considered the old Paul dead, gone, crucified with Christ on the cross and the new life he now lived, he lived in faith through Jesus.

People who witnessed this radical transformation were at first skeptical and confused by this new Paul, but the old Paul was gone and this new Paul began to travel the countryside telling everyone he met they too could be transformed... born again into this new life.

To be a follower of Jesus is to be a new creation. This is not about a new feature, a new formula, a new color, or even new packaging...we are talking a new creation.

Old things have passed away...all things have become new.

We should be lining up for this...

---

[205] Acts 23:6

68 - Mercy

To have mercy or to be merciful is to show compassion or extend forgiveness to those you have the power to punish or harm. The powerful are in no need of mercy. It is the powerless, the weak, or the defenseless that must plead for mercy.

Mercy is the antidote to judgment.

Matthew 18 tells a mercy-full story of a servant who owed a very large sum of money to his king. He could not pay this debt, so the king ordered the man, his wife, his children, and all of his belongings to be auctioned off at the slave market. The man then threw himself on the mercy of the court and pleaded for another chance to pay back his debt. The king, so moved by the servant's impassioned plea, erased the debt completely and set him free.

However, as the servant left the court, he encountered a fellow servant who owed him a very small sum of money. He demanded this fellow pay him immediately. The poor servant begged for mercy, but instead the forgiven servant had him arrested and thrown in jail until he could come up with the money to repay him.

When the other servants witnessed this, they were appalled and immediately reported this event to the king. The king had the servant brought back into court and then proceeded to vent his outrage over how having just been forgiven a huge sum of money this servant could have a fellow servant thrown into jail over such a minuscule debt. The scripture tells it this way.

"Then his lord summoned him and said to him, "You wicked slave! I forgave you all that debt because you pleaded with me. Should you not have had mercy on your fellow slave, as I had mercy on you?""[206]

Needless to say, the king was not amused and handed the servant over to be *"tortured until he would pay his entire debt."*[207]

As Christians we are not immune to behavior similar to that of the forgiven servant in the story. Oftentimes, we are the more than willing recipients of God's mercy while at the same time the less that generous dispensers of mercy to those around us. When we attempt to place ourselves in the role of judge and jury, we reveal the extent to which we have misinterpreted and misunderstood the Gospel and our role in the story.

God alone sits in judgment and we are powerless to do anything other than throw ourselves on the mercy of the court. God's sentence has been pronounced. Our verdict is that of...forgiven. As such, followers of Jesus should be mercy-full in a world that is more often than not, mercy-less.

---

[206] Matthew 18:32-33
[207] Matthew 18:34

69 - Listen

Listening seems like such a basic skill, but many of us find it harder and harder to listen as the noise level in our lives gets louder and louder. This is not so much a loudness in the typical sense, but is instead a loudness that comes to us in the form of to-do lists, texts, tweets, updates, traffic, radio, television, cell phone etc. From the moment we get up in the morning until the moment we fall asleep we are surrounded with this noise. Many of us have gotten so dependent on the noise that we can not get to sleep without the sound of electronically generated ocean waves or crickets to lull us to sleep. Its no wonder in conversations with friends, co-workers and even family members we get the question: "Are you listening to me?" Oftentimes it is best not to answer that question truthfully?

You would think if God wanted to speak to us in the midst of all this noise, that God, the creator of the universe, the one who spoke creation into existence would speak to us with a voice that commanded our attention...a voice that echoed off distant galaxies...a voice we couldn't help but listen to. But scripture tells us this is not the case.

"Then he [Elijah] was told, "Go, stand on the mountain at attention before God. God will pass by." A hurricane wind ripped through the mountains and shattered the rocks before God, but God wasn't to be found in the wind; after the wind an earthquake, but God wasn't in the earthquake; and after the earthquake fire, but God wasn't in the fire; and after the fire a gentle and quiet whisper."[208]

---

[208] 1 Kings 19:11-12

The voice of God is not a loud thunderous voice that commands our attention; it is in contrast a *gentle and quiet whisper*...a whisper that can easily get lost in the noise of our lives.

To hear this whisper we must pay attention, we must listen intently, we must turn down the noise. The more we attempt to listen, the more often we will hear. And, the more often we hear, the more easily we will be able to recognize the voice of God above the noise of our lives. Followers on the trail of Jesus are good listeners.

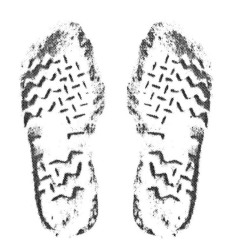

70 - Life

Breath is that which separates the living from the dead. As long as you are breathing, you are alive. But the moment your chest ceases to rise and fall, life on this earth has left you. This is how life was understood for centuries. But, Jesus arrived on the scene talking about a new kind of life...a spirit life...a kingdom life...an eternal life. Naturally people were curious.

Much of Jesus' teaching was about how to live this new eternal life...this new kingdom life. The possessors of eternal life were expected to live their lives quite a bit differently than those who embraced the cultural understanding of what constituted a good life. This new life turned the old life upside side down. This upside down life was perhaps best explained in Jesus' Sermon on the Mount.

In this message, Jesus proclaimed what it means to be blessed in this upside down life. He said you will be blessed when you are poor in spirit, when you mourn, when you are meek, when you hunger for righteousness, when you are merciful, when you are pure in heart, when you are a peacemaker, and when you are persecuted for the sake of righteousness.[209] All of this would likely have been a rather hard sell if it were not for the miraculous events happening in association with Jesus and this new life. Lives were being changed. Diseases were being cured. The blind were now able to see. Many individuals were the recipients of this new life.

The exclamation point on this new life story took place in a stone tomb outside of Jerusalem. A crucified Jesus was placed in the tomb and a fully alive Jesus emerged...a living example of this new eternal life. Jesus told everyone,

---

[209] Matthew 5: 3-11

"I came so they can have real and eternal life, more and better life than they ever dreamed of."[210]

Christians are the recipients of a new life...an upside down life...for the breath of life that left Jesus as he hung on the cross returned to him in a tomb as he began to breathe in the rarefied air of the eternal kingdom in which we now live. Being a follower on the trail of Jesus is all about life...a new life in the eternal kingdom of God.

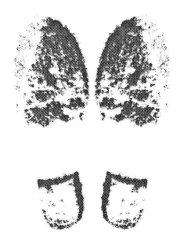

---

[210] John 10:10 (The Message)

71 - Gospel

Just as the essence of Jesus can be expressed in *the Word*, the story of Jesus' life, message, crucifixion, and resurrection can be summed up in *a word*...the Gospel. In a literal sense, the word *gospel* means *good news*. In a Christian context, the Gospel means the good news of Jesus Christ. This good news was apparently so good and so big that a single telling was not enough since the canon includes four tellings of the story we now know as the Gospel. Matthew, Mark, Luke, and John each tell their stories in an attempt to clarify that which became clear to them...Jesus is the living Word of God...the Messiah.

Their stories tell of a miraculous life. They tell a message for all ages. They tell of a crucifixion more horrible than we can imagine. But, most importantly they tell of a resurrection...a resurrection that brings the dead back to life.

Without the resurrection, the Gospel is historical. Without the resurrection, the Gospel is another set of principles on which we can use to give meaning to our lives. Without the resurrection, the Gospel is another sad story of a good person who came to a tragic end.

But with the resurrection, the Gospel moves out of history and into eternity; the Gospel gives a message of hope to those trapped in despair; the Gospel provides the cross on which our sin can be nailed; and the Gospel becomes a resurrection in which we all can participate.

The Gospel is indeed a story too big for a single telling and like Matthew, Mark, Luke and John, as followers of Jesus, we too must tell our story as we attempt to clarify for others that which has become clear to us... Jesus is the living Word of God...the Messiah... and this Gospel is indeed good news!

72 - Faith, Hope, Love

Faith is a kind of trust or confidence in something. In Christianity, our belief in Jesus is sometimes called our faith in Jesus: our confidence in Jesus and his promises.

Hope is inspired by faith. Hope is the expectation that some future event will come to pass. Our faith places our eyes on the horizon of hope. But, love is a different animal altogether.

Chapter 13 of 1 Corinthians is oftentimes called the love chapter. In it Paul paints a picture of what it means to love.

"Love is patient; love is kind; love is not envious or boastful or arrogant or rude. It does not insist on its own way; it is not irritable or resentful; it does not rejoice in wrongdoing, but rejoices in the truth. It bears all things, believes all things, hopes all things, endures all things. Love never ends."[211]

Love is a position. Love is an action. Love is a way of living. Love is infinitely more than a way to express our affection for people or things. Paul states that if he speaks in tongues, has the gift of prophecy, and has the faith to move mountains…if he does not have love *"it profits me nothing."*[212] Paul concludes the discussion of love with the following.

"And now faith, hope, and love abide, these three; and the greatest of these is love."[213]

It is easy for one to have faith without love. It is also easy for one to have hope without love. But once we start attaching words like Christian to our faith and

---

[211] 1 Corinthians 13:4-8
[212] 1 Corinthians 13:3
[213] 1 Corinthians 13:13

our hope, love must take up permanent residence within us and manifest itself in our approach to others. Faith, hope, and love are all part of what it means to be a follower of Jesus, but *the greatest of these is love.*

73 - Embodied

There are parts of the country where the following phrase is pretty common: "Boy, you are the spittin' image of your father." Or, "Girl, you are the spittin' image of your mother." This phrase is not limited to providing genetic accolades to your parents. It can also be used in reference to your aunt or uncle or brother or sister… but it is hopefully not in reference to someone outside the known gene pool for this could cause more than a little "spittin."

But, how in the world did that phrase come to be…you are the spittin' image? Did someone spit just like some one else? Seriously; sometimes language is just a mystery. However, in spite of its seeming randomness, we do know what they meant. They were saying there is something about you; your looks, your behaviors, your stance, your speech patterns, whatever, but something about you reminds them of someone else or in other words; they see the image of someone else in you.

It is likely no one ever said this to Joseph (Jesus' earthly father), "Joseph, that Jesus, he is just the spittin' image of you." How could they, Jesus had another father…something that could have broken up the family and left us with a different story to tell, but it didn't. Jesus was, however, the spittin' image of someone else and Jesus was the one to point this out.

"Philip said to him, "Lord, show us the Father, and we will be satisfied." Jesus said to him, "Have I been with you all this time, Philip, and you still do not know me? Whoever has seen me has seen the Father. How can you say, "Show us the Father'? Do you not believe that I am in the Father and the

Father is in me? The words that I say to you I do not speak on my own; but the Father who dwells in me does his works."[214]

Jesus was more than the spittin' image of God, Jesus was God, the physical manifestation of God on this earth. Talk like this is what got Jesus crucified and it continues to be a stumbling block to people today.

To be embodied or to be an embodiment of something you must "be an expression of or give a tangible or visible form to an idea, quality or feeling."[215] Jesus was indeed the embodiment of God. This is miraculous enough all by itself, but it does not end there. As Christians, we are to be the embodiment of Jesus. Paul puts flesh on the idea of this embodiment though the Body of Christ metaphor.[216] He tells us as Christians, we become the arms, hands, legs, feet, and all the various supporting organs that give life to the Body of Christ on this earth. Paul says, *"The body we're talking about is Christ's body of chosen people. Each of us finds our meaning and function as a part of his body."*[217] Christians are not only a part of the Body of Christ; we find our meaning, our purpose, and our life as part of this body. Followers of Jesus are to embody Christ, to be the spittin' image of Christ, to give visible form to the Savior on this earth. We have no greater calling.

---

[214] John 14:8-10
[215] http://oxforddictionaries.com/definition/embody?region=us&q=embodied
[216] Romans 12
[217] Romans 12:5

74 - Communion

Here are a couple of definitions for the word *communion*.

- "The sharing or exchange of intimate thoughts and feelings"[218]

- "The idea of common participation"[219]

Each definition contributes to our understanding, but neither of them begins to address the degree of intimacy contained within the Christian understanding of the word communion.

When the word communion is used in a Christian context, it becomes an intimate connection to the point of oneness…of no separation…a merging of the many into the one. We need look no further than the Trinity for an example of communion in this theological sense for the essence of the Trinity…the Father, Son & Holy Spirit is an intimate communion of three in one…the three aspects of God in a common-union…a communion.

While celebrating the Passover with the disciples on the night of his betrayal, Jesus took his relationship with the disciples to another level.

"While they were eating, he took a loaf of bread, and after blessing it he broke it, gave it to them, and said, "Take; this is my body." Then he took a cup, and after giving thanks he gave it to them, and all of them drank from it. He said to them, "This is my blood of the covenant, which is poured out for many.""[220]

---

[218] http://oxforddictionaries.com/definition/communion?region=us&q=communion
[219] Bromiley, *Vol. 1*, 752.
[220] Mark 14:22-24

This partaking of the bread and wine is commonly called communion for in it we celebrate not only Jesus' sacrifice but also our becoming one with him. Some within the Church believe the bread and water become the actual body and blood of Christ when we celebrate communion. Others prefer to see the elements of communion as more symbolic or metaphorical. In either case, this sacred practice serves to remind followers of Jesus of the communion with God we now enjoy.

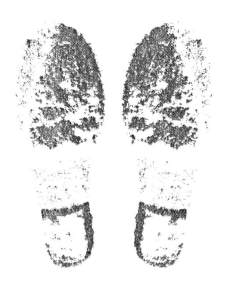

75 - Blood

There are not many things more traumatic as a child than suffering an injury that causes bleeding for blood is the unquestionable evidence of something more that a boo-boo. Blood means we are in trouble. Blood means life is draining from our bodies. Blood means…go get mom or dad…quick.

Once mom or dad arrives on the scene they wash out the wound and apply pressure to stop the bleeding. In severe cases, there is a trip to the emergency room when the injury is above mom or dads pay grade or when stitches can do what Band-Aids cannot.

While we may not believe it at the time, the blood spilling from our wound is not just an unfortunate consequence of our injury; it has a greater purpose. It washes out the wound and then clots to form a protective covering…stopping the bleeding and sealing the wound. In spite of its traumatic overtones, this natural process is in fact a good thing that works to bring about our healing.

In 1876 Robert Lowry wrote a song about the healing power of blood that is now a Christian classic called *Nothing But the Blood*.

What can wash away my sin?

Nothing but the blood of Jesus;

What can make me whole again?

Nothing but the blood of Jesus.

(Chorus)

Oh! precious is the flow

That makes me white as snow;

No other fount I know,

Nothing but the blood of Jesus.

While bleeding from an open wound as a child, we would not have called the blood flowing from our injury precious. However, in Christianity, Christ's blood is indeed most precious as it brings about not only our healing but also our redemption.

As we grow into adulthood, when our spirits are injured or we suffer some sort of soulful abrasion, we don't call out for mom or dad to help us. Typically, we try to take care of these wounds ourselves as we attempt to salve our spirits; possibly denying they happened or burying these traumas deep where no one can see them. While these attempts may obscure our injuries from public view, they only serve to encourage our wounds to fester and infect our lives and the lives of others in ways we never imagined.

Followers of Jesus have learned, or are learning, that healing can only occur when we abandon our attempts to heal ourselves and instead allow Jesus' blood to wash over and through us, cleansing our wounds and bringing about the healing we desperately need.

What can wash away my sin?

Nothing but the blood of Jesus;

What can make me whole again?

Nothing but the blood of Jesus.

76 - Welcome

While most of us likely think of ourselves as friendly, there are some who seem to rise above the crowd with a gift for making everyone feel welcome and at ease. You know who they are. They are the ones who have never met a stranger. And, they are typically huggers...much to the dismay of people who are not quite so free with their personal space.

If any collection of people should be known as welcoming, it seems like it should be Christians. However, research reveals this is not the verdict in the court of public opinion. David Kinnaman and Gabe Lyons discovered "the three most common perceptions of present-day Christianity are antihomosexual (an image held by 91 percent of young outsiders), judgmental (87 percent), and hypocritical (85 percent)."[221] That does not sound very welcoming.

If this is in fact the case, we have strayed a great distance from the manner in which Jesus approached humanity. Jesus was not afraid to touch the lepers or dine with the tax collectors. He claimed as his own those who society had excluded from the circle of acceptability...those who lived their lives in the midst of a culture that kept its welcome at a distance. It was Jesus who accepted them. It was Jesus who welcomed them into fellowship. It was Jesus who gave them hope.

If we are to be the arms and legs of Jesus, we should use these arms to welcome and these legs to locate us in the presence of those who live at the fringes into the fellowship of Christ. Followers of Jesus should be welcoming

---

[221] Kinnaman and Lyons, *Unchristian*, 27.

huggers and "space" invaders, as we are enactors of the love of Jesus in the world.

"So reach out and welcome one another to God's glory.

Jesus did it; now you do it!"[222]

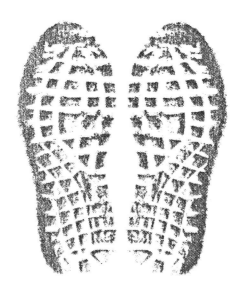

---

[222] Romans 15:7

77 - Justified

In a court of law, one can be exempted from the guilt and punishment associated with committing some act when their actions are considered justified, meaning they are exempted from the punishment their actions might otherwise deserve.

Theologically speaking, as followers of Jesus, we are considered exempt from punishment resulting from our sins due to the fact that we have been justified or exempted from the penalties for these sins through our faith and the sacrifice of Jesus on our behalf.

Interestingly, this understanding has not always been the case since the doctrine of justification, historically, tended to vacillate between faith as the sole source of justification, or faith with the addition of good works as a requirement for justification.

This dilemma was the subject of much angst for Martin Luther as he struggled with being good enough for God. It was only when he stumbled upon the revelation that he was justified by faith via the grace of God, apart from his own efforts, that he was able to fully embrace his redemption. Here it is in Luther's own words:

> "My situation was that, although an impeccable monk, I stood before God as a sinner troubled in conscience, and I had no confidence that my merit would assuage. Therefore I did not love a just and angry God, but rather hated and murmured against him. Yet I clung to the dear Paul and had a great yearning to know what he meant [in Romans].

Night and day I pondered until I saw the connection between the justice of God and the statement that "the just shall live by his faith." Then I grasped that the justice of God is that righteousness by which through grace and sheer mercy God justifies us through faith. Thereupon I feel myself to be reborn and to have gone through open doors into paradise."[223]

This revelation undergirded and fueled Luther's efforts to reform the church in the 16th century, leading to his nailing 95 Thesis to the door of a church in Wittenberg launching what we know today as the Reformation.

Justification is a gift from God through faith. There is no distinction between you and me and monks of old, we have all fallen short of God's glory and intended purposes for our lives...therefore our only hope for justification lies in the gift of grace enabled through the shedding of Jesus' blood. In the end, judgment will be pronounced. However, our penalty has been paid in Christ as we are justified through faith in Him. Celebrating this is entirely justified.

---

[223] Roland H. Bainton, *Here I Stand: A Life of Martin Luther* (New York: Meridian, 1995, 1950), 49.

78 - Self-Sacrifice

Many of us have multiple personalities disorder…sort of. By this I mean we live our public lives in ways that present an image of who we want to be or who we think we should be while at the same time doing our best to obscure a reality that can oftentimes be quite different. This difference doesn't have to be something dark or sinister. It could be something as small as refusing dessert when having lunch with friends in order to give the impression of being health conscious all the while knowing we are going to consume a pint of premium ice cream when we get home. Or, it could be something more serious as evidenced by the many falls from grace that appear in the news when public personas collapse under the weight of private realities.

Christians are not immune to this malady. We oftentimes find ourselves being pulled in different directions as we try to live our lives somewhere in between Christ's call to self-sacrifice and the primary myth of Western culture: the one who dies with the most toys wins. Pursuing this dualistic path typically necessitates the segmenting of our Christian life to Sundays or whenever it is convenient so as not to get in the way of our quest for the "good life."

At the root of this issue is the conflict between our embrace of Jesus' sacrifice without our also embracing the self-sacrifice that goes hand in hand with this calling. Clinging to Jesus with one hand while attempting to grab for the "toys" with the other, more often than not, leaves us either ineffective at both or pulled apart in the process.

Jesus never said the life of a disciple would be easy.

"He called the crowd with his disciples, and said to them, "If any want to become my followers, let them deny themselves and take up their cross and

follow me. For those who want to save their life will lose it, and those who lose their life for my sake, and for the sake of the gospel, will save it. For what will it profit them to gain the whole world and forfeit their life?"[224]

None of us will be able to carry our cross casually with one hand while keeping our other hand free to raid the cookie jar. Cross carrying requires our full attention. Cross carrying requires self-sacrifice. Cross carrying requires both hands. Followers on the trail of Jesus are those who hands are firmly affixed to the cross.

---

[224] Romans 8:34-36

79 - Imperfect

Those who are masters in the fine art of shopping understand what discovering an imperfection in an item means when shopping... it means the item is flawed and a discount may be available to the shrewd negotiator. Even though this imperfection may be small or nearly imperceptible, it is nonetheless, an indicator that the item is not worth full price. While this rule may apply in shopping, it lies in direct opposition to the message of the Gospel.

The Bible tells us, while we were originally created in the image of perfection, our current situation finds us some distance from that description: we are damaged goods.

Some of us bear the visible scars of our imperfections as the toll life has extracted from us is easily revealed on our faces, or the circumstances of our lives. In the rest of us, our imperfections may not be quite so visible as we have grown proficient at concealing or obscuring them from public view. But, in both and all cases, we humans have imperfections...we are flawed...we are indeed damaged goods.

Fortunately, Jesus did not come to here to save the perfect, he came for the imperfect, the down-trodden, those who find themselves cast aside on the highway of life unable to get back up and face the world in their imperfect state.

In our futile attempts to hide our scars, to act as if everything is ok, to hide our imperfections as a way to show we are good enough, we should bear in mind the price that was paid for us. Our imperfections did not allow us to be bought at a bargain price. Our imperfections necessitated we be bought at the highest price; Jesus' sacrifice on the cross. While in our humanness we remain imperfect, in God's eyes, followers of Jesus are restored to his intended vision of perfection through Jesus.

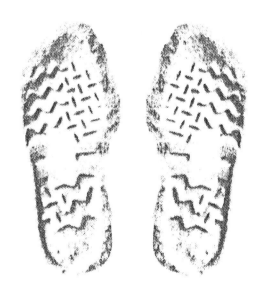

80 - Baptism

Baptism is part of the Christian experience; we accept Christ and are then baptized with baptism serving as a sign, a public proclamation of our new life in Christ. Few would argue with this understanding of baptism. But, before we get too comfortable with it, consider this?

"John the baptizer appeared in the wilderness, proclaiming a baptism of repentance for the forgiveness of sins. And people from the whole Judean countryside and all the people of Jerusalem were going out to him, and were baptized by him in the river Jordan, confessing their sins."[225]

John was baptizing before Jesus arrived on the scene. He was known as John the Baptizer for goodness sakes. He even baptized Jesus. So, if we are to suggest baptism is symbolic of our new life in Christ, what was going on here?

Ceremonial water purification was pretty common in ancient Israel as water was used to make that which was unclean, clean again. Even Aaron had to be washed (cleansed) before putting on his priestly robes: *"Moses brought Aaron and his sons forward, and washed them with water."*[226] So, John's baptism echoed these ceremonial washings, signifying the need for a moral cleansing, a confession of one's sins, and repentance.

Jesus was even baptized by John, which is interesting since Jesus was one without sin. This would lead us to believe John's baptism of Jesus was perhaps symbolic of Aaron's ceremonial cleansing before taking on the role of priest, as Jesus was himself about to take on the role of priest in a new kingdom.

---

[225] Mark 1:4-5
[226] Leviticus 8:6

John, however, did not proclaim his baptism as anything other than a preparation for the baptism that was yet to come. *I baptize you with water; but one who is more powerful than I is coming; I am not worthy to untie the thong of his sandals. He will baptize you with the Holy Spirit and fire."[227]* In the same way that Jesus amplified and raised the standards of The Law with the Sermon on the Mount, Jesus brought baptism into its fullness.

"Go therefore and make disciples of all nations, baptizing them in the name of the Father and of the Son and of the Holy Spirit, and teaching them to obey everything that I have commanded you. And remember, I am with you always, to the end of the age."[228]

[227] Luke 3:16
[228] Matthew 28:19-20

81 - Journey

A journey is different than wandering. When we wander we have movement but we are not headed toward any place in particular. A journey is not for those headed no place in particular. A journey is for those headed toward a destination. As followers of Jesus, we are on a journey toward a particular destination. We are on a journey toward a New Kingdom. We are on a journey toward eternity.

Many paths are available to those on this journey. This is made evident by the variety of stories in the Bible of those who have gone before us. Their stories tell of the joys we will encounter on the journey but they also tell us of the pitfalls that await us if we stray too far off the path, which we inevitably seem to do. These stories tell us that God's word is a lamp unto our feet and a light unto our path.[229] This is good news for there are most assuredly times when we will think the darkness is too dark and our journey too difficult to continue on.

But we should be encouraged because we do not make this journey alone. Not only do we have our fellow travelers with whom we share stories of New Kingdom sightings along the way, but we are also accompanied by the truth of our destination...by Jesus. Followers of Jesus are indeed on a journey. It is a journey with a destination. It is a journey with Jesus toward eternity.

---

[229] Psalm 119:105

82 - Cast Off

There are two kinds of people in this world...those who love garage sales and those who don't.[230] To those who love garage sales, these intersections of private capitalism and house cleaning provide an opportunity to sell or purchase unwanted items for a fraction of their original value.

"Hmmmm. Seventy-five cents for that shirt? You've got to be kidding. I'll give you twenty-five cents and not a penny more."

"Sold!"

For the rest off us, garage sales can seem like a sad affair as those things that used to have value and meaning in someone's life are displayed on the driveway in an effort to exchange them for cash so they can go buy new things, things that will likely face the same fate in a few years when they, once again, do a little deep house cleaning.

Living life as a follower of Jesus typically involves a little personal house cleaning when we find ourselves in possession of unwanted attitudes or destructive behaviors we no longer want or need in our lives. When this happens, it is time to do a little casting off.

We may have to cast off the idea that we are the center of our universe as we begin to align ourselves with the center of all things. We may have to cast off the belief we are somehow better or superior to those who happen to sin in a different way than we do. We may have to cast off our security so we can engage in missions in far away lands, or we even may need to cast off our

---

[230] Ok, maybe a slight exaggeration, but...

insecurities as we try to figure out how to love our neighbors as ourselves. In any case, being a Christian involves a lot of casting off.

However, in this process of casting off, we are not placing these unwanted items in the driveway in hopes of selling them so we can acquire new items that will ultimately need replacing someday. Instead, we are casting them off in pursuit of that which has the most value...life as a follower of Jesus.

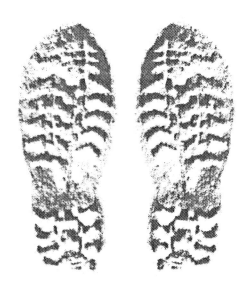

83 - Harmony

If you have ever attended the performance of a symphony orchestra, hopefully you arrived early enough to hear the orchestra tune up. While the process of tuning does not succeed in commanding the attention of the audience, nor is it usually followed by an uncontrollable burst of applause, to miss the tuning is to miss what is arguably the most critical element of their performance.

Tuning typically begins with the oboe as it plays a single reference note to which the entire orchestra tunes. As this note is played, each member of the orchestra checks their instrument and makes adjustments to bring it into harmony with the reference tone. Thirds, fifths, and octaves bounce off one another as this unscripted wall of sound crescendos and then gradually resolves into a properly tuned orchestra. When the tuning is over, they are ready to perform the composer's masterpiece.

After intermission, the orchestra typically repeats this tuning ritual. The untrained observer might question the necessity to repeat the process since they just tuned at the beginning of the program. However, the seasoned musician knows that environmental factors such as heat, humidity, or even the playing of the instrument itself necessitates the need for re-tuning.

Christians, as members of the Body of Christ, are similar to the musicians in an orchestra. We each have our individual parts to play in God's masterpiece. To play these parts as they were meant to be played, we need to be in tune...in harmony...with the reference tone of God echoing throughout creation.

Environmental factors or maybe even just life itself can cause us to drift out of tune, so, just like the members of the orchestra, we too must re-tune so that we can remain in harmony for the performance of our lives.

Followers on the trail of Jesus know that to remain in harmony with God they must be in a near constant state of re-tuning.

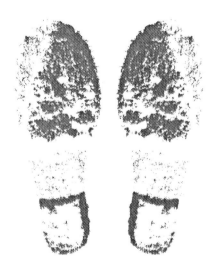

84 - Hope

Most of us are familiar with a certain series of movies that tell stories of a long time ago in a galaxy far, far away. In the first one of these films, a princess goes to extreme measures to save her people by sending a message in hopes that it would reach its intended recipient.

"Help me Obi Wan Kenobi, you're my only hope."[231]

Ultimately, her message made it to Obi Wan and, well, I don't want to ruin the ending for you. [232]

In life, we can place our *hope* in many things: in ourselves and our abilities, our circumstance, our finances, and other people. However, hope placed in these things is often hope misplaced as we can let ourselves and others down, our circumstances can change, our finances can evaporate, and others can betray us.

In spite of all this, we are called to live in hope...a hope that takes physical form in the person of Jesus Christ. To do that we must send out a message;

"Help us Jesus, you're our only hope."

---

[231] Star Wars
[232] As if you haven't seen the movie. :)

85 - Peace

Most of us have seen one of those photos of planet Earth taken from space. In this image we see the continents, we see the oceans, we see what for all practical purposes appears to be a beautiful peaceful planet. However, as we all know, this peaceful mirage disappears at ground level. Wars rage on nearly every continent. Personal addictions entrap and enslave. Children that used to be able to roam the neighborhoods playing until exhaustion brought them home now grow up in gated communities to avoid becoming the targets of those who find themselves the purveyors of destruction.

There are many things to worry about...seemingly more every day. As a consequence, anxiety medications fly off the shelves of the pharmacies in record numbers as many of us attempt to medicate some peace into our lives. But peace on this Earth does not come out of a bottle or is it found behind the walls of an urban fortress. Peace is found in the presence of God.

Paul speaks of a peace that is available to those of us who take up residence in the Body of Christ.

"Do not worry about anything, but in everything by prayer and supplication with thanksgiving let your requests be made known to God. And the peace of God, which surpasses all understanding, will guard your hearts and your minds in Christ Jesus." [233]

Paul's prescription can be a tough pill for many of us to swallow in our search for peace...peace in the news we just received from our soon-to-be ex-spouse, peace in the less than good news from our oncologist, peace in the

---

[233] Philippians 4:6

call from our child's teacher saying they suspect some sort of substance abuse is contributing to our child's academic decline. Peace in this world is under constant assault.

But, the prescription is clear. Through prayer we are to lift up our concerns to God. As a result we will find ourselves living in the peace of God. This peace will be hard for many to understand because it is a peace that will manifest itself in the midst of the trials of our lives. It is a peace that will baffle those around us who might misinterpret this peace as a lack of concern when we don't join them in a worry filled existence. However, it is a peace for which we all long, and a peace that will draw others toward the trail as followers of Jesus.

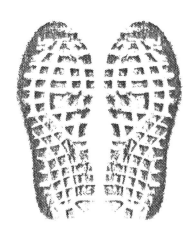

86 - Pray

Prayer is a common practice within communities of faith. It is an intentional act in which we focus our attentions on God. Many times our prayers consist of running through a laundry list of concerns and requests. This is valid and is one of the purposes of prayer. But, some of our most important prayer time is spent in silence...in silent anticipation of the still soft voice of the Holy Spirit that whispers life into the depths of our souls.

Jesus tells us when we pray, we should pray in private[234] and that our prayers should not be filled with many words for *"Your Father knows what you need before you ask him."*[235] And, there we have one of the more curious instructions in the Bible. We are compelled to pray; to bring our requests before the Lord, in spite of the fact that he knows what we need before we ask him.

So, if God knows what we are going to ask before we ask, why then do we pray?

First of all, we spend time with those that are important to us. We spend time with our spouses, our children, and our friends. When we intentionally spend time with them we are telling them they are important. There does not have to be an agenda associated with the time together. We spend time with them because we want to be with them. They are a priority to us. In the same way, when we spend time with God in prayer, we are letting God know that He is important to us, that we want to be with Him, that He is a priority in our lives.

---

[234] Matthew 6:6
[235] Matthew 6:8

And as is true with our spouses, children, and friends, we are a lot more fun to be around if we are not talking all the time. We are more fun when we both talk and listen. When we talk all the time we are telling the other person we are more important than they are... our stories are funnier than theirs...that we are primarily interested in ourselves. When we talk all the time we will likely find the list of people who enjoy spending time with us diminishing in number. People tend to enjoy the company of those who are good listeners rather than good talkers.

God is a good listener. He wants to hear the issues that weigh heavily on our hearts. But, when we stop talking and begin to listen, when we let God talk, we get to hear the issues that weigh heavily on God's heart. Prayer is the way in which God's concerns become our concerns.

Followers of Jesus are good listeners.

87 - Fruit

Fruit is a common metaphor in the Bible. It is so common, one might be tempted to consider it the primary metaphor, for almost everything, at some point, seems to get related to fruit.

Initial references to fruit in the Bible have to do with actual tangible fruit: fruit of the trees (Genesis 3:2), fruit of the ground (Genesis 4:3), fruit of the womb (Genesis 30:2), fruit of your labor (Exodus 23:16), fruit of the land (Numbers 13:20), fruit of your livestock (Deuteronomy 28:4), fruit of vineyards and olive yards (Joshua 24:13) and fruit in its season (Psalm 1:3).

From this literal understanding of the word fruit, the Bible moves to a different kind of fruit; fruit that is a consequence of our actions: the fruit of the righteous (Proverbs 11:30), the fruit of the mouth (Proverbs 12:14), the fruit of their words (Proverbs 13:2), the fruit of their hands (Proverbs 31:16), the fruit of their schemes (Jeremiah 6:19), the fruit of their doings (Jeremiah 17:10), and the fruit of lies (Hosea 10:13). Fruit manifests in many forms.

As we continue on in the story, we read that *"every tree therefore that does not bear good fruit is cut down and thrown into the fire."*[236] And that *"each tree is known by its own fruit."*[237] While these verses tell us there are consequences to the production of less that good fruit, the following verse reminds us, the point of our efforts is not the fruit, but instead, that our good fruit brings honor and glory to God. *"My Father is glorified by this, that you bear much fruit and become my disciples."*[238]

---

[236] Matthew 3:10
[237] Luke 6:44
[238] John 15:8

But, what kind of fruit are we to bring about? What is the good fruit? Paul answers this question for us in Galatians when he tells us of a different kind of fruit...a fruit of the spirit. *"The fruit of the Spirit is love, joy, peace, patience, kindness, generosity, faithfulness, gentleness, and self-control."*[239]

So, being a follower on the trail of Jesus does involve some gardening; some spiritual gardening, as we direct our efforts toward producing the good fruits of the Spirit, for these are the fruits that produce a harvest of glory for God.

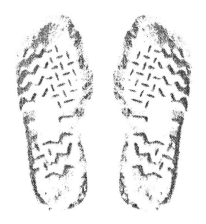

---

[239] Galatians 5:22-23

88 - No

No is not a word we like to hear. When we ask for something, we are not typically asking in hopes of getting a *no*. We are asking in hopes of getting a yes. Sometimes, when a yes is not forthcoming, we ask the question over and over in hopes the person will eventually tire of saying no, and we will get our yes.

While children are very good at this strategy, interestingly, *no* is one of the first words they learn in an effort to exert a little control in their lives. Do you want some more peas? No. Do you want to take a nap? No. Do you want to go to the store with me? No.

The ability to say *no* gives us control. The ability to say *no* gives us options. The ability to say *no* enables the existence of love.

Wait...what did I just say? That's right. The ability to say *no* enables the existence of love for without the ability to say *no*, love is not love, for real love is a voluntary affection.

Our ability to say *no* to God is problematic for many people since it makes possible a future in which we can spend eternity apart from God. But, it is this ability to say no to God that enables love between God and man to exist. The ability to say *no* enables the existence of love.

"For God so loved the world, that he gave his only begotten Son, that whosoever believeth in him should not perish, but have everlasting life."[240]

Whosoever implies the ability to say *no*. Whosoever is an invitation to anyone. Whosoever makes love possible.

When God asks the question: will you love me? He is hoping for a yes. It is not a one chance and one chance only question, for God will continue to beckon us into His love again and again and again, in hopes we will eventually tire of saying no and

eventually

say

yes.

God's love is enabled in the no, but finds fulfillment in the yes.

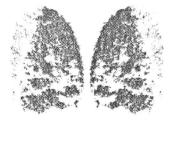

---

[240] John 3:16 (KJV)

89 - Three

The easy way to approach the word *three* in our book of signs would be to tie it to the *three* members of the Trinity; Father, Son and Holy Spirit, and leave it at that. But, to do so would be to miss the importance of the way the word occurs throughout the Bible. We discussed "threes" when we talked about the Trinity in Signpost #11, but lets dig a little deeper, think a little harder, and take a closer look at motifs.

Motifs are symbolic.

Motifs are connective.

Motifs reveal greater meaning.

Motifs are found in movies when a musical theme is associated with a particular character in the film. Motifs are found in literature when a recurring theme connects events or words as a way to convey greater meaning. Motifs are found in art when an element echoes that of another piece or style.

Motifs are the connective tissue that link individual elements to a greater story. The word "three" is a motif that is symbolic, connective, and reveals greater meaning. A simple Bible word search for the word *three* reveals the following occurrences.

Old Testament

• The number of men that appeared to Abraham informing him that he would have a son. (Genesis 18:1-2)

• The number of days Moses told Pharaoh they must travel into the wilderness to worship God. (Exodus 3:18)

• The number of days of darkness that fell over Egypt when Moses stretched out his hand toward heaven. (Exodus 10:22)

• The number of guys who defied Nebuchadnezzar's order to worship his statue and were subsequently rescued from the fiery furnace. (Daniel 3)

• The number of days Jonah spent in the belly of the whale. (Jonah 1:17)

New Testament

• The number of months the newly pregnant Mary stayed with her cousin Elizabeth. (Luke 1:56)

• The number of wise men who came to find Jesus. (Matthew 2)

• The number of gifts these wise men brought. (Matthew 2)

• The number of days a young Jesus remained in the temple talking with the teachers. (Luke 2:36)

• The number of people who passed by the injured man in the parable. (Luke 10:36)

• The number of days the hungry crowd had been with Jesus with nothing to eat. (Matthew 15:32)

• The number of things that should manifest in our prayers to God. *"Ask, and it will be given you; search, and you will find; knock, and the door will be opened for you."* (Luke 11:9)

• The number of times the cock crowed before Peter denied Jesus. (Matthew 26:34)

• The number of days it would take Jesus to rebuild the temple. (Matthew 26:61)

- The time of day Jesus cried out on the cross saying " *"Eli, Eli, lema sabachthani?" that is, "My God, my God, why have you forsaken me?"* (Matthew 27:46)

- The number of days Paul was without sight after his blinding. (Acts 9:9)

This is in no way a comprehensive list, but these instances help reveal a motif: the symbolic significance of the number *three* in the Biblical narrative. And what is this motif? Threes in these stories seem to connect these events to the miraculous presence of God. But, the usage of this motif also reveals something else: this motif occurs in both the Old and New Testaments, foreshadowing that which was present and yet to be revealed: our understanding of God as a Trinity: Father, Son, & Holy Spirit.

And so, in this motif of threes, not only do we find symbolism, connection, and greater meaning, we also find a God who will go to the greatest of lengths to reveal His presence with us, then, now, and in the future that stretches out before us as followers of Jesus.

90 - Peculiar

Did you ever notice how the scents or aromas from certain foods can fill the house and linger for days? Fried foods can do this, as can foods involving garlic or bacon. They fill the space with a smell that is *peculiar* to that particular food...a smell that has an *exclusive relationship* or *connection* to its source.

"But ye are a chosen generation, a royal priesthood, an holy nation, a peculiar people; that ye should shew forth the praises of him who hath called you out of darkness into his marvellous light."[241]

The original Greek word that is translated here as peculiar is the word περιποίησιν or peripoiēsin which means a *possession*[242] or *for acquisition.*[243] Later translations do not use the word peculiar, but rather they translate peripoiēsin as "God's own people" (NRSV), "God's instruments" (The Message), and "a holy nation" (NIV) to name a few. In this sense, followers on the trail of Jesus are citizens of a holy nation, chosen by God as God's instruments on this earth, those whose presence fills the air with the peculiar aroma of God, the scent of the one who sent us. Followers of Jesus are a peculiar people.

---

[241] 1 Peter 2:9 (KJV)
[242] http://interlinearbible.org/1_peter/2-9.htm
[243] Young, *Young's Analytical Concordance to the Bible*, 737.

91 - Full

The Gospels bookend Peter's experience with Jesus in stories of fullness. In the first, Peter (then Simon) had been out fishing all night with nothing to show for it when along came Jesus suggesting Peter, once again, let his nets down in the water. With slight protest, Peter lowered the nets, which nearly filled to the point of breaking with fish. Peter signaled for their fishing partners to help them and both of their boats became so full of fish, they almost sank. Peter's response was curious.

"When Simon Peter saw this, he fell at Jesus' knees and said, "Go away from me, Lord; I am a sinful man!"" [244]

Now, lets fast forward approximately 3 years later, post crucifixion and resurrection. Once again we are told a story of Peter fishing as Peter apparently does: all night fishing with nothing to show for it. An unrecognized Jesus, standing on the shore said to them: *""Cast the net to the right side of the boat, and you will find some." So they cast it, and now they were not able to haul it in because there were so many fish."* [245] All of a sudden Peter had a revelation. He knew what this meant. He had experienced this before. This time however, rather than asking Jesus to depart, Peter leaped into the sea and swam as fast as he could to Jesus on the shore.

Same people, same story, different endings.

In the first story, a full net brought Peter's emptiness to the surface.

---

[244] Luke 5:8
[245] John 21:6

In the second story, a full net brought Peter into the presence of his friend and savior: Jesus.

Peter had learned to read the signs. He had learned the true meaning of the sign. A full net like this meant Jesus was near.

The Bible says Jesus was full of the Holy Spirit,[246] while also being full grace and truth.[247] Signs that reveal the presence of this fullness of spirit, grace, and truth can bring us to our knees. They can also inspire us to action, compel us to change directions, and perhaps, even cause us to abandon safety and security to fling ourselves into the sea (metaphorically of course), so that we might be found in the presence of Jesus.

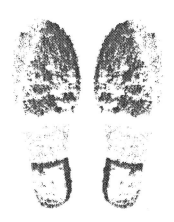

---

[246] Luke 4:1
[247] John 1:14

92 - Sinner

The idea that we are sinners in need of a savior seems to have fallen out of favor in post-modern culture. As post-moderns, we much prefer to worship at the altar of individualism while embracing a plurality of truth claims of which no single claim finds itself particularly privileged.

This myth of post-modernity lies in contrast to one of the primary truths revealed in the Gospel...the truth that we are all sinners in need of a savior...in need of Jesus. This raises a question: how have we, as a culture, gotten to the point where sin has lost its sting in a smorgasbord of individual choice? Perhaps it is because truth needs to be revealed rather than explained.

When John the Baptist wanted to determine if Jesus was the Messiah, he sent his disciples to find out. They asked Jesus:

"Are you the one who is to come, or are we to wait for another?"[248]

Jesus responded:

"Go and tell John what you hear and see: the blind receive their sight, the lame walk, the lepers are cleansed, the deaf hear, the dead are raised, and the poor have good news brought to them. And blessed is anyone who takes no offense at me."[249]

The evidence of Jesus identity was not contained in an explanation but rather a revelation. "The truth of Jesus' identity was found in what he did, not in the beliefs he claimed to embrace." [250]

---

[248] Matthew 11:3
[249] Matthew 11:4-6
[250] Ingram, *The New Normal,* 224.

As followers of Jesus, if we are to in some way help elevate the truth of Jesus over and above the other lesser truths, we must privilege the way and life of Jesus as the manner in which we make his truth known: living truth rather than explaining truth. Truth lived is better than truth told.

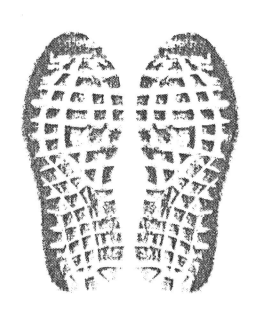

93 – Word & 94 - Glory

In one of its usages, "word" is a shortened form of the phrase "my word is my bond" which originated within the inmate population of American prisons.[251] Essentially, it means "truth." [252] For example, if someone were say The Book of Signs was a great book, you might respond "word." :)

In the Bible, John introduces us to Jesus as the living Word of God.

"In the beginning was the Word, and the Word was with God, and the Word was God. He was in the beginning with God."[253]

Word is the English translation of the word *logos* used in the original Greek New Testament and has a variety of interpretations. The pre-Socratic philosopher Heraclitus (circa 500 B.C.) used the term to express "an underlying coherence or principle of the universe."[254] The Stoics used logos in a variety of ways to express true reason, the source of ideas or growth, expressed reason, or immanent reason (unexpressed thought.)

John continues:

"And the Word [the logos of God] became flesh and lived among us, and we have seen his glory, the glory as of a father's only son, full of grace and truth."[255]

---

[251] http://www.urbandictionary.com/define.php?term=Word
[252] http://www.urbandictionary.com/define.php?term=Word
[253] John 1:1
[254] Bromiley, *The International Standard Bible Encyclopedia V4*, 1103.
[255] John 1:14

The word *glory* can have many meanings, but in this sense we can take it to mean worshipful praise, a distinguished quality, great beauty and splendor, and a state of gratification or exaltation.[256]

So, if we look at this verse in the context of these meanings of glory, we can see Jesus as the Word (logos) of God existing in a state of worshipful praise, displaying distinguished qualities with great beauty and splendor in an attitude of gratification and exaltation of God... his Father...full of grace and truth.

It is hard to read John's words without sensing the almost breathless manner in which he is making this proclamation. It is as if he can hardly wait for us to understand, to grasp what he is trying to tell us...the reality that God in human form has not only walked the earth but has changed the trajectory of humanity for all who will accept and believe this truth. For followers on the trail of Jesus, these are indeed glorious words to which we can all respond... "word."

---

[256] http://www.merriam-webster.com/dictionary/glory

95 - Metaphysical

Christianity is not likely the first thing people think of when they hear the word *metaphysical*. In fact, a quick Internet search for metaphysical reveals topics dealing with healing, peace, crystals, and gurus, but precious little reference to anything *metaphysical* from a Christian perspective.

The word metaphysical is the combination of two words...*meta* and *physical*. *Meta* is originally a Greek word meaning *"with, across, or after."*[257] But as is true with most words, meaning tends to change over time. Currently the word *meta* denotes a position *"behind, after, or beyond"*[258] or *"something of a higher or second order kind."*[259] And of course, *physical* refers to those things that are tangible or concrete. So if we combine *meta* and *physical* to make metaphysical, we get a word that refers to *"the transcendent or to a reality beyond what is perceptible to the senses."*[260] From a Christian perspective, the word metaphysical would seem to relate directly to our understanding of what it means to be Christian. This is especially true if we connect some dots...

Revelation records God making the following statement.

"I am the Alpha and the Omega," says the Lord God, who is and who was and who is to come, the Almighty."[261]

God is the Alpha and the Omega...the beginning and end...the One who is, was, and is to come.

---

[257] http://oxforddictionaries.com/definition/meta-?region=us
[258] Ibid.
[259] Ibid.
[260] http://www.merriam-webster.com/dictionary/metaphysical
[261] Revelation 1:8

God is *with*, *across* and *after*.

God is *behind*, *after* and *beyond*.

God is beyond that which is *perceptible to the senses*.

While the world may want to exclude God from the metaphysical, if anyone or anything ever was metaphysical, it is God. Actually, for it to to be more accurate, if someone were to look up the word metaphysical in the dictionary, maybe it should just say...*see God*.

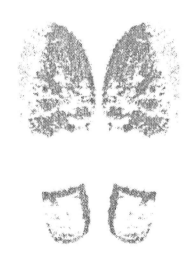

96 - Create

There is a story that goes something like this. After years of research, a group of scientists believed they now understood how life on earth was created and therefore could duplicate the process. In the bravado of their claim, they issued a creation challenge to God; which God accepted. As the challenge began, the scientists reached down to grab a hand full of dirt. God objected and told them: "Hey, get your own dirt."

The dirt in the joke is of course in reference to the creation story in Genesis 2.

"The Lord God formed man from the dust of the ground, and breathed into his nostrils the breath of life; and the man became a living being."[262]

In addition to revealing a creation methodology, this passage provides us with at least three insights into the way in which God creates. First of all, God does not create from a distance but instead is present with his creation. Second, God is not afraid to get his hands dirty to bring creation into existence. Third, God is intimate with creation as he comes close enough to breathe life into its nostrils. These are three of the ways in which God approaches creating.

In the redemptive work of Jesus, we see a similar creative trajectory. First, Jesus does not act from a distance but instead walks with creation at street level. Second, Jesus is not afraid to get his hands dirty as he touches the untouchable, befriends the friendless, and gives hope to the hopeless. Thirdly,

---

[262] Genesis 2:7

Jesus takes on the sins (the dirt) of humanity in order to breathe new life into God's creation…a born again kingdom creation.

Many times, as followers of Jesus, we are tempted to remain behind the protective walls of the sanctuary; keeping our distance from the untouchables of our culture; delegating the birthing of a born again creation to the professionals we hire to do the dirty work for us. But, this strategy is not consistent with the creation narrative or the message of Jesus.

Creating requires us to leave that which is safe so that we can engage life at street level. Creating is a dirty business and requires getting our hands dirty. Creating is done face to face.

Following Jesus is hands on, in your face, dirty business, but it is the creation life those on the trail of Jesus must imitate if they are to draw closer to him.

97 - Until

Until is an interesting word for our book of signs since it does not identify a specific trait or thing associated with what it means to be Christian, it merely identifies the space we must occupy until something happens. Until is an anticipatory word. It points to some time in the future.

When we are anticipating a future event, we count down the days *until* it happens.

Expectant parents wait anxiously *until* the birth of their child.

Travelers question how long *until* they arrive.

We are among the world of the living *until* our chests cease in their rising and falling.

Until implies an anticipation of some future event.

Until implies that we are not yet fully formed.

Until implies that we have not yet arrived.

Until implies that we are still of this world.

But, we are not left alone in this ontological world of in-between. While we live with an expectation of that which is yet to be, to miss the present is to miss the meaning of life. True, our calling is to live with expectancy of that which is to come, but our mission is also to bring a little of that *until* world into the present. The Lords Prayer reminds us of this when it says *"Your kingdom come. Your will be done, on earth as it is in heaven."*[263] The doing of the will is done in the present.

Follower of Jesus are those who embrace and live into the until.

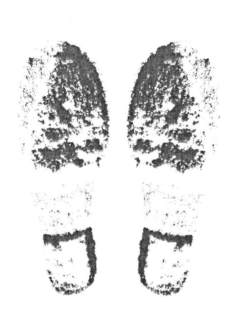

---

[263] Matthew 6:10

98 - Suddenly

It is interesting that the word *suddenly* follows the word *until* in our book of signs for many times our seasons of *until* come to an end *suddenly*. Suddenly suggests something unexpected, unimagined, unforeseen, or unanticipated. Oftentimes, God acts *suddenly*.

Suddenly the heavens opened up and the spirit of God descended as a dove. (Matthew 3:16)

Suddenly Moses and Elijah appeared talking to Jesus. (Matthew 17:3)

Suddenly there was an earthquake when an angel descended from heaven to roll away the stone. (Matthew 28:2)

Suddenly a sound like a rushing wind filled the house and the disciples began to speak in tongues. (Acts 2:2-4)

Suddenly a light from heaven blinded Paul and he heard the voice of Jesus. (Acts 9:3)

Suddenly there was an earthquake that freed Paul from prison. (Acts 22:6)

As followers of Jesus attempting to live out our lives in the *until*, we should keep the following in mind.

Situations can change *suddenly*.

Hearts can be restored *suddenly*.

Directions can be changed *suddenly*.

And, hope can be restored *suddenly*.

99 - Giving

Give	Hugs
	High fives
	Handshakes
Give	Birthday presents
	Anniversary presents
	Christmas presents
Give	Encouragement
	Advice
	Support
	Hope
	Peace a chance
Give	To those in need
	Of ourselves
	Our time
But never	Give up
	Give in
	Give out

Followers on the trail of Jesus are giving...

100 - Odd

In his book, The Black Swan, Nassim Nicholas Taleb suggest our preference for studying outcomes that are the most likely, the usual, the events that occur at the top of the bell curve...what we might call normal events, is misguided because, as he puts it, "normal is often irrelevant."[264] Taleb does not mean to imply that normal events are without consequence, but that normal can be completely disrupted by the unexpected; that which is odd or out of the ordinary. As such, he suggests our time is better spent studying and focusing on the unexpected, the odd; what he calls Black Swan events.

The title of Taleb's book, The Black Swan, refers to a belief that endured for many years...a belief that all swans were white...a belief that was confirmed by the empirical evidence...[265]right up until the point black swans were discovered in Australia. For Taleb, this shift in awareness serves to illustrate the fragility of our knowledge when it is based strictly on observations and experience.[266]

Drawing upon this and many other examples, Taleb suggests three attributes of a Black Swan event:

- The event lies outside that which is expected.

- The event is impactful.

---

[264] Nassim Nicholas Taleb, *The Black Swan: The Impact of the Highly Improbable* (London: Penguin, 2008), xxiv.
[265] Ibid., xvii.
[266] Ibid.

• We tend to explain away its uniqueness as a way to make it appear less random.[267]

When those in ancient Israel first heard the stories about Jesus, it probably sounded a little odd: a virgin birth, water into wine, healing blind eyes with spit and dirt, feeding thousands with a few fish and a few loaves of bread, a dead man rising to life, an unwarranted crucifixion, and a resurrection...to name a few. Everyone who heard the stories or witnessed the events had a decision to make: ignore them, explain them away, work against them, or try to understand their significance in the world and for their lives. History tells the stories of their choices.

Today, the stories about Jesus can also seem pretty odd to a post enlightenment mind, perhaps even odder as we are removed by distance, time, and culture. None-the-less, they still demand a decision from us.

• Do we choose to ignore them.

• Do we try to explain them away as sleight of hand or perhaps fables for another time.

• Do we try to work against them, promoting life strategies that stand in stark contrast to that which Jesus advocated.

• Or, do we try to understand them, to make sense of them, to do our best to integrate them into our lives.

Nothing about following Jesus will be ordinary. It will be extra-ordinary. It will be challenging. It will be rewarding. It will be the adventure of our lives.

It's an odd way to change the world...very odd indeed.

---

[267] Ibid., xvii-xviii.

Afterword

A couple of things…

For more information on the theological justification for crowdsourcing please check out a series of articles I wrote for Patheos.

http://www.patheos.com/blogs/evangelicalpulpit/2015/01/on-whose-authority-do-we-crowdsource/

Or, my chapter titled Every Bush is Burning in Signs of Life, edited by Brian Ross.

For more information on my work visit www.thomaseingram.com

Email: tom.ingram@mac.com

Bibliography

Atkerson, Stephen E. *House Church - Simple-Strategic-Scriptural*. Atlanta: New Testament Reformation Fellowship, 2008.

Attridge, Harold W., ed. *The HarperCollins Study Bible: Fully Revised and Updated*. Rev Upd ed. San Francisco, Calif.: HarperOne, 2006.

Bainton, Roland H. *Here I Stand: A Life of Martin Luther*. New York: Meridian, 1995, 1950.

Block, Peter. *The Answer to How Is Yes: Acting On What Matters*. San Francisco, CA: Berrett-Koehler Publishers, 2003.

Bromiley, Geoffrey W. *The International Standard Bible Encyclopedia: Vols. 1-4*. Grand Rapids, MI: Eerdmans Pub Co, 1995.

Funk and Wagnall's New Comprehensive International Dictionary of the English Language. Deluxe reference ed. Newark, N.J.: Ferguson Pub, 1982.

Holstein, James A., and Jaber F. Gubrium. *The Self We Live By: Narrative Identity in a Postmodern World*. New York: Oxford University Press, USA, 1999.

Ingram, Dr. Thomas E., *The New Normal: a Diagnosis the Church Can Live With.* Tulsa: Linen Publishing, 2014

Kelly, Kevin. *The Inevitable: Understanding the 12 Technological Forces That Will Shape Our Future*. New York, New York: Viking, 2016.

Kinnaman, David, and Gabe Lyons. *Unchristian: What a New Generation Really Thinks About Christianity-- and Why It Matters*. Grand Rapids, Mich.: Baker Books, 2007.

Lakhani, Karim R., and Jill A. Panetta. "The Principles of Distributed Innovation." *Innovations: Technology, Governance, Globalization* 2, no. 3 (2007): 97-112.

Lewis, C. S. *God in the Dock: Essays On Theology and Ethics*. Grand Rapids, MI: Eerdmans Pub Co, 1994.

Nouwen, Henri J M. *Reaching Out: The Three Movements of the Spiritual Life*. Garden City, N.Y.: Image Books, 1986.

Owram, Doug. *Born at the Right Time: A History of the Baby Boom Generation*. Toronto: University of Toronto Press, Scholarly Publishing Division, 1997.

Page, Scott E. *The Difference: How the Power of Diversity Creates Better Groups, Firms, Schools, and Societies (New Edition)*. Princeton: Princeton University Press, 2008.

Rezendes, Paul. *Tracking and the Art of Seeing: How to Read Animal Tracks and Sign*. 2nd ed. New York: HarperCollins, 1999.

Rollins, Peter. *Insurrection*. Nashville, Tenn.: Howard Books, 2011.

Rokeach, Milton. *The Three Christs of Ypsilanti*. New York: NYRB Classics, 2011. Kindle ebook.

Russell, Bertrand. *RC Series Bundle: Power: A New Social Analysis (Routledge Classics)*. New York: Routledge, 2004.

Taleb, Nassim Nicholas. *The Black Swan: The Impact of the Highly Improbable*. London: Penguin, 2008.

Trumball, H. Clay. *The Covenant of Salt*. New York: Charles Scribner's Sons, 1899.

Unger, Merrill F. *The New Unger's Bible Dictionary*. rev. and updated ed. Chicago: Moody Press, 1988.

Yoon, Carol Kaesuk. *Naming Nature: The Clash between Instinct and Science*. New York: W.W. Norton, 2009.

Young, Robert. *Young's Analytical Concordance to the Bible*. Peabody: Hendrickson Publishers 01/01/, 2005.

Web Based Bibliography

AMC Movies - http://www.amc.com/movie-guide/50-greatest-romantic-movies

Concordance - http://concordances.org/greek/3101.htm

CNET - http://news.cnet.com/2100-1038_3-5997332.html

Crowdsourcing Theology - http://www.crowdsourcingtheology.com/crowdsourcing_theology/100_Words.html

Geert Hofstede - http://www.geerthofstede.nl/culture/dimensions-of-national-cultures.aspx

Geert Hofstede - http://www.geerthofstede.nl/research--vsm.aspx

Ideascale - http://www.ideascale.com

Innocentive - www.innocentive.com

Interlinear Bible - http://www.interlinearbible.org/

Psychological Science - http://www.psychologicalscience.org/index.php/news/releases/your-spouses-voice-is-easier-to-hear-and-easier-to-ignore.html

T. Aubin, P. Jouventin, and P. Hildebrand, "Penguins Use the Two-Voice System to Recognize Each Other.," *Proceedings of the Royal Society B: Biological Sciences* 267 (2000): 1081-87, accessed January 22, 2015, http://www.ncbi.nlm.nih.gov/pmc/articles/PMC1690651/.

Mayo Clinic - http://www.mayoclinic.org/healthy-living/nutrition-and-healthy-eating/in-depth/water/art-20044256?pg=1

Mayo Clinic - http://www.mayoclinic.org/diseases-conditions/dehydration/basics/symptoms/con-20030056

Mirriam-Webster Dictionary, http://www.merriam-webster.com

Money - http://money.usnews.com/careers/best-jobs/rankings/the-100-best-jobs

Oxford American Dictionary, http://oxforddictionaries.com

Rice University - http://www.rice.edu/~jenky/sports/salt.html

Statista - http://www.statista.com/topics/1156/coupon-market-trends-in-the-united-states/

Strong's Concordance, http://concordances.org/greek/3101.htm

Urban Dictionary - http://www.urbandictionary.com/define.php?term=Word

U.S. Department of Energy - http://energychallenge.energy.gov

Bible Quotations and References

Appendix A - Crowdsourcing Contributors

- aliceworthit
- alissa.ingram
- andrewdavid
- asillis
- barb-sipe
- bill gibson
- bill prosise
- bo liles
- brenna
- brettdehart
- brian vallotton
- bridgekidssarah
- bruursema
- bwatson
- cajl33
- catpharm03
- charlenamiller09
- chauncey lattimer
- chris miller
- christopher.paul.abel
- cindymug
- claytonfaulkner
- clhardin
- clrampey
- cricket.keith
- cwillz
- dan.brown
- daniellehartland
- david banks
- david Phillips
- dbuckle
- derek white
- dertbiker2000
- dladuke7
- docharris
- drews
- dustinsells
- dvanbrakle
- eharout
- elle
- eric wilbanks
- ernie.flowers
- escofranks
- evangelistmatt
- expatminister
- fdhis
- fred knowlton
- george
- glmulkey
- gspastor
- harry
- haynes jeff
- hchapman
- iamtravis
- jacob
- jacquesb
- jasonveach
- jaygraffam
- jcfretts
- jefflincicome
- jenwatson5
- jfolsom
- jim Carlson
- jim.kane.jr
- jmlake42
- joanpball
- johndyer
- jonathan.a.mills
- jones8475
- joyhooper
- jwpratt585

- karl4life
- kdbullock
- kdove09
- kevin.satterlee
- kevinjmontgomery
- lataya ballard-simpson
- lauramcdd
- ltkerns
- margaret Burbank
- matt
- mattryananderson
- mhasty
- miguel horacio
- Molson
- mwkruse
- mwxtodd
- partofthejourney
- pastor donna
- pastorbeetle
- paul rose
- paulivany
- petervey
- postmodernnegro
- preachermom41
- randevick
- rawhite2
- retracmj
- revanne
- revdad27
- revmatt
- revray01
- robert fuller
- rooney
- russ
- sandy cathcart
- scottb
- seanwitty
- singingtree123
- slw3stacy
- sherwoo
- stephenbedard
- steve corn
- stevewiltjer
- strickland00
- thebalkes003
- thegoodings2
- thyrkas
- tony
- tshepherd1
- umpastorstuart
- valharvard
- vern
- wally
- wclegg
- westfound
- william
- wjohnson14
- wvcnpastor

Field Notes

Use this section to make note of signs you have discovered on the trail of Jesus.

You can add your notes to the ongoing discussion at the following link:

www.crowdsourcingtheology.com and click on the "signs" tab.

Field Notes

Field Notes

Field Notes